THE DREAM INTERPRETERS

Which One or None?

To Bobby
with Love from
your sister. xxx
Steph (Aden)
July 2019

THE DREAM INTERPRETERS

Which One or None?

DR STEPH ADAM

Published by Dr Steph Adam

A CIP catalogue record for this book is available from the British Library.

ISBN 978-1-5262-0758-6

Book layout and design by Clare Brayshaw

Cover illustration by Stuart Trotter

Production by:

York Publishing Services Ltd
64 Hallfield Road
Layerthorpe
York
YO31 7ZQ

Tel: 01904 431213

Website: www.yps-publishing.co.uk

For my two daughters, Rachael Adam and Sarah Adam,
who have filled my life with joy, and given me countless reasons
to be a very proud mother.

Contents

Preface

Dreams are fascinating as they allow us to cross a threshold into a previously unchartered area of our sleeping mind, with the possibility of providing us with new perceptions. A moment of such enlightenment is often referred to as the switching on of a mental light bulb, when an obscure experience suddenly becomes crystal clear.

Experiences like these were rare when as a counsellor I struggled professionally to make sense of my clients' dreams. This was because I couldn't find a compatible theory to suit my way of working. I therefore entered a Doctoral research programme and investigated all the dream theories which have emerged during the past hundred years. The results from this research and my new theory for humanistic practitioners, are outlined in my thesis held at the University of Manchester.

As I wanted the general reader to benefit from my research I selected five of the most important dream theories and simplified their techniques for personalised dream interpretation. These theories have equal strengths and limitations to identify meanings from dreams. However, relying on one approach does limit the information we extract from dreams and the messages that they are trying to communicate. I believe that an understanding of dreams, to increase knowledge about ourselves, can only be achieved with the integration of the strengths from various approaches.

I have combined features of these approaches to produce a new theory, which examines all aspects of human experience in your dream world and transfers them to your waking world. By linking dreams to current events this provides a deeper understanding of the emotional side of your life and encourages you to make appropriate waking life changes.

You can choose which theories you prefer to use by interpreting your dreams alongside the dream journals shown as appendices. I recommend that people who experience night-terrors or post-traumatic stress disorder should consult a doctor before trying out the techniques in this book. I hope you will find this resource helpful in understanding your dreams.

Acknowledgements

This book didn't get written without the support of many people. In particular, I wish to thank my editor Alison Williams (https//alisonwilliamswriting. wordpress.com). Alison's skilled editing, and ability to weed out superfluous information helped me to transform the original manuscript from an incoherent mess, into an accessible tool that you may find helpful to interpret your dreams. I want to give a big thank you to Duncan Beal and Clare Brayshaw of York Publishing Services who guided me through the self-publishing process. I owe a lot to Lizzi Linklater, Associate Lecturer for Creative Writing at the University of York. Lizzi enabled me to shake off academia and to write in a more friendly style for you, my readers. My thanks also go to The Gestalt Journal Press for allowing me to cite extensively from one of Fritz Perls' case studies, along with Headline Publishing for granting me permission to quote from *The Hound of the Baskervilles*. I would especially like to thank Rachael Adam for carrying out numerous edits and giving me valuable feedback, and Sarah Adam for patiently amending some of the illustrations each time I changed my mind. I am extremely grateful to Barbara Lambert who came to see me for a holiday, and got enlisted into helping out with some of the illustrations. I wish to thank a former love, Chrissy Gilham who listened endlessly to me talking about the different theories, and shared my life and dreams for many years. I am indebted to photographer James McHugh (https//yorlifephotography.com) who managed to capture my look of happiness (back cover), when this book became finished. Finally, I must pay tribute to all the dream researchers, psychologists, and psychiatrists who feature in this publication. Without their distinguished work to refer to, it would not have been written.

York, June 27 2018
Steph Adam.

List of Figures

List of Tables

1

Setting the Scene

My breathing feels rapid. I can't see anything, and I'm unsure where I am. Suddenly, a glimpse of a fleeting memory emerges from the murky recesses of my mind. I realise that I'm in the halfway house between the two states of sleeping and waking. I recall the following dream:

> I'm near a white block of flats frantically looking for Nora. She's disappeared (2012).

Despite my best efforts to hold onto the above image it evaporates like disappearing fog. Busy brain cells try to regain control of the situation by telling me to remember more. I can't, and what unravels is a growing sense of confusion as to what my dream is about. My bewilderment is short-lived, and I don't think too hard to work out the meaning of this dream. It reveals to me that I'm in a familiar waking neighbourhood, anxiously searching for my pet terrier Nora, who died in waking life nine years earlier. This dream is a reminder of the loss of a much-loved dog, and it's an immediate understanding of the uncomplicated imagery that allows me to reach a meaning so quickly. The dream presents no unusual characteristics, and portrays a realistic scenario of the kind of events which take place in my waking world.

This is not the case with most of my dreams. I have puzzled over my unusual dreams ever since I was fifteen when I dreamt of my grandad dressed as my headmistress telling me, 'Everything will be ok'. My grandfather's presence in the dream showed him as a kind figure, but also as a strict headmistress. I realised later in life that he was referring to my troubled situation at the Carlisle and County High School for Girls. I narrowly escaped expulsion for appearing in a photograph taken by a *Daily Express* photographer.[1] The photograph showed me and eighty other girls waving our arms in a militant manner, protesting against wearing our berets correctly. I, and most of the other pupils, wanted to wear our berets on the backs of our heads like plates, to avoid ruining our hairstyles.

Thinking about this dream at the time paved the way for me to do something formal about discovering the meaning of dreams later in my professional life. As a former counsellor, when clients came to the sessions I became drawn into the "mystery" of the dream scenarios they presented. This had a detrimental effect on the therapeutic relationship, as I could only nod in acknowledgement to their dream story, and felt disempowered to work effectively.

Because of my limited knowledge on this subject, I completed a Doctoral study[2] at the University of Manchester during 2003–2009. Given that the subject of dreams and therapy in the UK is sparse, my study investigated the usefulness of clients discussing their dreams in therapy. As a result of my research, I found it was helpful for clients to discuss dreams as a way of promoting personal growth and facilitating change in their waking lives. Due to the personal knowledge that dreams bring, it's also beneficial for general readers to explore their dreams for the same reason.

A Definition of Dreaming

The place to start the discussion on dreams is to try and define what they are. Dreams are considered enigmatic and hallucinatory (illusive) and are part of human experience throughout recorded history. Their meanings remain a hotly contested topic as it's difficult to describe the subjective variety of dreams. Dreams are mainly a visual experience which occurs when we are asleep. They craft a story-like quality which features us as an observer, and sometimes as a participant. We are usually located in a setting which may be familiar, with objects, and other characters who interact with us and each other. These features of dreams are known as the "content", which are borne out of individual narratives that lead to previously hidden meanings. The content of dreams is relatively unaffected by the immediate external environment, as dream events unravel at the whim of the dreamer. Information is less restricted due to an absence of rules which dictate the social norms, and events are accepted without remorse or conscience. These occurrences happen because we don't evaluate our dream experience against a backdrop of previous history. All these conditions result in dreams seeming bizarre when compared to the way in which we make sense of our waking life experience.

The content features are different to the "form" of dreams which describes the universal aspects. By that I mean every dream has the same structure. A useful analogy to highlight this difference is, a row of terraced houses represents the form, while each individual house represents the content. I will come back to explain the differences in more detail in Chapters 5 and 6.

One of the great advantages of exploring dreams is that they are completely honest, as they do not deceive us. In waking life we are often blinkered about our true thoughts and feelings. It therefore makes sense to try and discover the meaning of our dreams, to get to our true emotions, and how these impact on our waking life relationships and situations.

The Nature of Reality

Dreams have two realities. They consist of perceptions of characters and objects which appear real to us while dreaming, but on waking, we convert our dream experience into an unreal world, and question the authenticity of our dreams. The seventeenth-century philosopher Descartes adds fuel to the dilemma of reality with his famous "dream argument". He reports while remembering a dream as he sat by a fire in his room, he felt the heat from the fire in the same way as he felt it in his waking life.

Waking perception

For a moment, imagine Descartes' incoming sensory perception when sitting by a fire in his waking life:

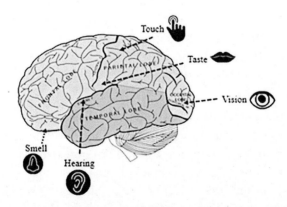

Figure 1.0 Descartes' Waking Perception[3]

To understand any incoming sensory information consisting of: vision, hearing, smell, touch, and taste, from the outside world, Descartes needs to process his thoughts. Thinking is generally referred to as a cognitive process, which is a mental activity that includes problem solving, intellectual reasoning, learning and memory. Descartes sees the fire while dreaming. It is reasonable to assume that he hears the wood crackling and can smell the wood burning, because a seventeenth-century wood fire is open. He feels the heat from the fire, and the only sense that's missing is one of taste. The other senses filter the incoming stimuli into the relevant parts of Descartes' mind, to give an internal reality of his outside waking world.

Dreaming perception

Now, back to Descartes' dream. In this mind all his senses are processed internally without reference to his outside world, with no reality checks.

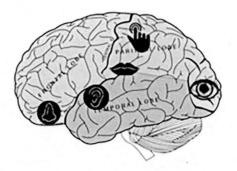

Figure 1.1 Descartes' Dreaming Perception[4]

While dreaming Descartes can see the dream, because he describes it to us. There is no dialogue, so he can't hear anything. The other senses of smell and taste aren't part of his experience. Feeling the heat from the fire while dreaming leaves Descartes with a problem. He can't believe the fire exists only in his waking world, and this prevents him from knowing whether he is awake or dreaming.[5]

This dream was one of the original sources for Descartes' argument of "methodical doubt". This thought experiment calls all our waking beliefs we have received from sensory perceptions to be considered as a deception. The kinds of examples he has in mind include the bent appearance of a straight stick when viewed in water, and the optical illusion of smallness created by distance. Because dreaming perceptions don't correspond to reality, then why aren't we more certain of our waking perceptions? How do we know that we don't exist in a continuous dream world?

While thinking about this problem, Descartes identifies one belief that resists all such attempts to deceive, the belief that he "exists". This debate which in its most famous form became, "I think, therefore I am" (known as the cogito). The argument is meant to be understood as follows: the very act of thought proves he existed, because he can't possibly think without existing.

What is truth?

Descartes speculates that, when he arrives at the certainty of recognising the cogito as true he calls it a clear and distinct perception. By showing that there is a truth which cannot be doubted, he established a stepping stone on which we can build a foundation for knowledge. Rather than relying on our doubtful perceptions, we can seek out clear and distinct perceptions that are within our own minds, then use our reason (logic) to acquire further knowledge from them.

The way in which we evaluate information by asking questions enables us to decide what is true and what is false. An objective truth claims that if we looked at a tree, another person looking at the same tree would perceive it in the same way. A more subjective view would consider that two people looking at the same tree may perceive it differently. These people may see different shapes, colours and so forth resulting in two equally valid interpretations of reality.

As you manoeuvre through the chapters you will likely find yourself yo-yoing between the opposite poles of doubt and certainty, and your thinking will be stretched by considering dreams in different ways. By asking yourself new questions about the facts I report, you may well continue questioning until you find your own reason – the place I call my reader's "truth".

A Brief History of the Meaning of Dreams

Early information about dream analysis comes from the Mesopotamian people, including the Sumerians who developed a system of writing on clay tablets. In about 2200 B.C.E. Gudea, a Sumerian king, preserved his dreams in this way. One puzzling dream tells of his search to find the meaning of a dream through a goddess, and this is one of the earliest illustrations of a connection between dreaming and the gods.

A history of dreams in Ancient Egypt dates to 2000 B.C.E. when the Egyptians wrote down their dreams on papyrus. Like the Mesopotamians, the Egyptians thought the gods communicated to them through dreams, which predict future events, and to offer suggestions for miraculous treatments for disease and injury. A second method of interpreting dreams was to have an A–Z dictionary, where each dream was cross-referenced to a symbol. Two collections of dream *omina* (special signs which appear in dreams) have survived, dating back to 2050–1790 B.C.E. They are known as the Chester Beatty Papyri, after the man who discovered them. They contain two hundred Egyptian dreams and are currently housed in the British Museum.

Artemidorus, a Greek philosopher, lived in the 2nd century AD and wrote a comprehensive encyclopaedia of five volumes about dream interpretation known as *Oneirocritica*.[6] He offers his readers a system and principles for categorising and interpreting dreams, believing that dreams could predict the future. These books contain a glossary of meanings and became a crucial influence on subsequent thoughts on dream interpretation.

By the time of the 4th century attitudes towards the meaning of dreams in Europe changed dramatically. A wealthy scholar, Saint Jerome, named Eusebius Sophronius Hieronymus at birth, wrestled with reconciling his interest in pagan classics with his studies of the Bible. He dreamt about how to resolve this issue – in his dream, he is taken before a heavenly judge and asked about his identity. Jerome claims he is a Christian, but the judge suggests he is a liar because he follows Cicero, a Roman philosopher, instead of Christ. The judge orders him to be punished by receiving many lashes. In waking life Jerome took an oath never to possess pagan books again.

After this dream Jerome was commissioned by Pope Damasus 1 of Rome to translate the Bible from Hebrew to Latin, later called the Vulgate. He deliberately mistranslated the Hebrew word *anan* for "witchcraft" which is considered a pagan superstitious practice. Jerome altered this word to read "observing dreams"[7] in three cases out of ten citations of the word. This meant the Hebrew text of "You shall not practice augury or witchcraft" was changed to read "You shall not practice augury or observe dreams." It may have been because of his dream that he tried to discourage others from pagan influences. Jerome issued a caution against observing false dreams, and people who discussed their dreams openly were often associated with witchcraft.

Adding to Jerome's scaremongering tactics, one of his contemporaries, Macrobius, issued a warning in his publication *Commentary of the Dream of*

Scipio.[8] He tells about the experience of nightmares, in which two dreaded demonic creatures appear. An incubus is a male demon who has sexual intercourse with women, often impregnating them with hell-spawned children. A succubus is the female equivalent who seduces male dreamers, ultimately taking their soul with her ravenous sexual appetite, which her victim is unable to resist. This book was one of the most well-known dream books in medieval Europe and influenced further hysteria about evil spirits.

Through the Dark Ages (AD 500–1500) dreams were viewed as immoral, with the Christian clergy becoming obsessed with sex and sin. Dream images were seen as a seduction from the devil attempting to lead dreamers down the wrong path. If women were naïve enough to divulge that they had sex with an evil dream character, they were often burned alive by the clergy.[9]

During the seventeenth and eighteenth centuries, dreams were finally freed from the restraints enforced upon them by the interrogating clergy, and they became disassociated from the devil. It's during this time that two schools of thought emerge, that dreams are caused by the physical factors of creating our mental being, or they reflect the dreamer's personality. Fast forward to the twentieth century, and in came the potential of dreams, which was about to be discovered through rigorous philosophical and scientific enquiry.[10]

Different cultural influences in dreaming

This book focuses on Western views of the meaning of dreams, and I explain the various techniques in the following chapters. However, I wish to acknowledge there are other cultural approaches such as the two I will presently describe which offer a flavour of different cultural philosophies.

Diverse cultural influences are continually observed by anthropologists studying alternative attitudes about the purpose and meaning of dreams. Iain Edgar, an anthropologist, refers to the work of Barbara Tedlock[11], who suggests that, when investigating other cultures' beliefs, the dream memory should extend beyond the recalled dream. It should include an explanation of different cultures' views regarding the purpose of dream-telling.[12] This is because the reason for the dream events taking place can influence the meaning of that dream.

For example, while dreams feature prominently in day-to-day decisions for the Aguaruna Indians of Peru, they don't have an individual hold on their perceptions of reality. Instead, dreams are experiences that disclose possibilities or events that are developing, rather than accomplished facts. Only when dreams are intentionally induced by eating psychotropic plants, such as Banisteriopsis (also known as datem), a South American hallucinogenic vine, do they have a bearing on practical activities.[13]

One report tells of a young man who was stricken by an inability to encounter game animals for hunting. After taking the hallucinogen datem in waking life, in a subsequent dream he witnessed many desirable species which had previously escaped from him. Shortly after having this dream his hunting ability was revived, and he claimed that by seeing the animals in his dream-like state, this brought about the cure.[14]

The Kagwahiv tribe from the Amazon in Brazil share their dreams which have their origins in a prophetic nature. A dream that appears unfortunate in its omen for the future is told quickly by the fire to eliminate its prediction. A favourable dream is told well away from the fire to ensure that its encouraging prediction may come true.[15] One account reports of a headman sitting in the middle of the settlement, away from the cooking fires. He told everyone within hearing about an erotic dream he had where he predicted a favourable forecast for hunting game.[16] The difference between these two dreams and the traditional Western view, is that the dreams are shared with their local community, and the tribe take seriously that dream messages are listened to, and adhered to.

One of the most debated scientific accounts concerning the cultural context of dreaming involves a Malayan tribe called the Senoi. They allegedly have a dream theory that is unlike anything in the Western world. This revelation was discovered by American psychologist Kilton Stewart, who learnt about it during his stay in Malaysia in 1934. He published his research regarding the Senoi dream theory in a paper called *Dream Theory in Malaya*,[17] which I will discuss in detail in Chapter 7.

Memory

The way to recall a dream is through memory, and it's the only connection we use as a resource between waking consciousness and access to tracing dreams. For the sake of clarity, I describe a model of memory which has developed from the information-processing approach.[18] Memory is represented as a flow of information that passes through a three-stage process sequentially: sensory memory, short-term memory (STM), and long-term memory (LTM).

Information is originally detected by the sense organs where it's registered for fractions of a second in sensory memory, before decaying or being passed on to STM. In the STM stage, information is stored for brief periods of time, which can be lost within thirty seconds unless transferred to LTM. Only if that information is repeated (rehearsed) will it be passed to LTM, otherwise it decays or will be displaced. Anything we need to remember for longer periods needs to be transferred to LTM which holds a vast quantity of information that can be stored for extensive periods of time. This information includes all our personal memories, our beliefs about the world, and our general knowledge, and can last almost a whole lifetime.

Most of us will experience some frustration in not remembering our dreams because dreams are invariably difficult to catch before they fade away. Many levels of physiological and psychological factors encourage as well as hamper our access to dream recall. One physiological possibility is that the neurochemicals in our brains are different to during waking time, and they don't allow us to consolidate our memories.

Whilst remembering dreams can be a difficult task, psychologically it's a skill that can be improved on and is essentially one of attitude. People who take their dreams seriously are more likely to recall their dreams than those who are sceptical. Memory images become the prime sources for the dream scenario, and when evaluating a dream from an awakening experience, extra ideas are added. As they aren't part of the original dream, we have accidently begun to interpret our own dreams.

Keeping a Dream Journal

I find the best time to recall a dream is just at the onset of waking from a full night's sleep. I recommend you keep your dreams in chronological order, and they should be reported uncensored to give them authenticity. After waking I usually record my dreams on my Dictaphone (this depends on where I sleep). I then transfer the dream report to my journal as soon as possible. One of the advantages of recording a dream is that we are more likely to catch it in its raw state. As this method is more immediate than thinking about what to write, we can produce a more accurate description for the original dream experience.

For those readers who wish to write down or record their dreams I advise that you use the first person, present tense such as, 'I am sitting in my lounge and…' This can give you a sense of re-living your dream and may help you to remember more. Before going to sleep I suggest you:

- Prepare an A5 folder with loose sheets which allows for reports to be added.

- Keep two pens, the A5 folder and a lamp by your bed.

On waking, ask yourself if you had a dream and do not open your eyes; lie still in the bed and try not to drift back off.

- Allow your mind to wander and let the images drift into your head.

- Open your eyes, gently sit up and switch on a light.

- Immediately write down or record a description of everything you remember.

- Record your thoughts and feelings as you awake.

- An option you may wish to consider is to draw your dream (Chapters 3 and 7).

- Give the dream a title in the same way that artists name their pictures (Chapter 7).

- Choose one of the journals to interpret your dream.

The above methods for reporting dreams are designed for personal use only and are for people who wake up naturally (not in a sleep laboratory).

The Post-Box Dream

Some of the typical inconsistencies that make it difficult to understand a dream are shown below in my post-box dream. I awoke feeling angry.

I'm in a department store where I used to work as an assistant store manager in my younger days. I want some lunch from the restaurant, but there is nothing left. I go into the kitchen and see a member of staff, Ann. She apologises because she is short-staffed. This makes me angry and I ask her to cook me some food. Then I take some documents which I want to post that are confidential. I don't want anyone to see them, so I shove them in a rucksack and leave the building. Next, I'm walking down a country lane and spot a red post-box, but I don't post the documents. I want a bus to come along as it's too far to walk. Then I see a country pub and go inside to get some food. It looks like a Chinese buffet, and the chef has ginger hair and a moustache. I ask him how much the buffet is, and he replies, '£23.99'. I think this is too expensive and say, 'It's daylight robbery', and we have a massive argument (2008).

The dream is reported from a chronological visual perspective as the events take place, and it shows a series of happenings pasted together like a collage, which causes the overall scene to appear irrational. This is the first problem that most of us encounter, trying to untangle a sequence of bizarre happenings.

Brigitte Booth, a retired Chair of Clinical Psychology at the University of Zurich, noticed in her studies that there's a difference in the way clients present their dreams to psychotherapists, from communicating everyday stories. She suggests when clients report their dreams, there's an absence of any kind of reasons why the events are taking place.[19] I believe the same process applies to the general reader when reporting their dreams. In my dream I don't explain the occurrences – it's almost as if I'm placed in the different dream scenarios by a magic wand.

Devoid of the insight and perceptions I use to evaluate my waking world, my dream can be described as "thin" by not having all these conditions present. This is the second dilemma that we face, by trying to identity perceptions and insights that are missing to create a narrative plot which makes sense.

Consequently, with the omission of a coherent plot, this dream story doesn't move forward to an obvious conclusion.[20] This is the third obstacle that we must overcome by identifying an ending to a dream.

After reviewing my dream, I have a list of questions as to how I can put the missing features back into my dream, and be able to determine an accurate meaning. The answers to these questions are given in Chapter 7, where I'll also explain how to use metaphor as an agent to analyse a dream.

Symbols and Metaphors in Dreams

Universal symbolism is found in dream dictionaries, and although they can give us a general idea as to what a symbol may mean, they can't tell us what that symbol means in the events of our specific dreams. Experts such as Ann Faraday[21], Clara E. Hill,[22] and Gayle Delaney[23] who have carried out research on dreaming, all agree that universal symbolism is misleading.

I agree with their views. However, there will be a few examples where symbolic imagery does contribute to dream meaning in this book, but only in the context of my dreams.

A metaphor is a figure of speech consisting of a word or phrase which is applied to something to which it isn't literally alike, and its purpose is to picture or explain something complex in straightforward terms. Delaney, a pioneer of using metaphor during the 1990s, suggests the dreaming mind resorts to the use of metaphorical imagery. This imagery can be likened to a CAT scan of a dreamer's psychological processes at a point in time.[24] Therefore, we must arrive at a conscious understanding of metaphoric language to understand our dreams if they are to have any impact on personal growth.

★ ★ ★

Before I outline my model, in Chapters 2–6 I explain the theories of Sigmund Freud, Carl Jung, Fritz Perls, Calvin S. Hall and Vernon J. Nordby and J. Allan Hobson. After reviewing all the theories, you can use the dream journals which are shown as appendices, and are individually adapted to suit these theories. Because dreams are so personal, I would like you to find new understanding about your dreams by yourself. A huge advantage of interpreting your own dreams in this way is that, with the right tools, your dreams can throw light upon personal meaning with complete accuracy. In Chapter 8, I carry out a summary of all the theories so that you can choose which theories you prefer. Finally, for those of you who wish to do so, in Chapter 9 there is an example of how to design your own model of dream interpretation.

## 2

Dreams Reflect the Fulfilment of Unsatisfied Wishes

Freud (1856–1939) is considered to be the father of modern dream interpretation and the most influential person to develop a psychological theory of analysing and interpreting dreams. Born in Freiberg which is now Příbor in the Czech Republic, he heard stories throughout his childhood that the old peasant woman who assisted with his birth prophesised that he was destined for fame.[1] This is because Freud entered this world with a caul (membrane) over his head, which was considered an omen of good luck. As Freud's mother believed in premonitions she called him, 'My golden Sigi,' favouring him over all her other children. This special treatment inspired him to strive towards professional recognition for the rest of his life.

Freud had a happy childhood. His parents encouraged a scholarly education and he graduated from school with honours, as well as being proficient in many different languages. At the age of seventeen, Freud briefly considered a career in law, but the lure of science was too strong. His interest in medicine was not only to cure, but also to use science as a seeker of the truth. Freud qualified as a doctor, after having worked in a several different departments in the Vienna General Hospitals, and eventually ended up in private practice.

In the winter of 1885, he went to Paris to consult with a famous neurologist, Jean Charcot who was treating patients with symptoms resulting from traumatic accidents. Charcot applied hypnosis to try to discover a technique which would distinguish between the symptoms of paralysis and hysteria (anxiety). Freud observed that some of Charcot's patients had symptoms for which there wasn't a physical cause, and he also noticed that their emotional difficulties soon disappeared when talking to Charcot under hypnosis. On waking, it seemed that the sessions had a positive effect on his patients' ongoing behaviour.

After returning to Vienna, Freud encouraged the use of hypnosis with his own female patients as a way of trying to cure their anxiety, and live a more beneficial lifestyle. He also dabbled in the use of cocaine to relieve his own hysteria, calling it 'euphoric and a wonder drug'.[2] Freud later administered cocaine for his friend Fleischl-Marxow, who became a morphine addict as a result of attempts to sooth the pain he suffered caused by an infection. This proved fatal; Fleischl-Marxow died a few years later. The death of his friend would haunt Freud in his famous dream of "Irma's Injection", which will be explained later in this chapter.

Freud's Theory of Personality

Freud continued to try and find a cure for hysteria, but his search didn't bring him the success he longed for. Instead it alienated him from his medical colleagues, and he consequently abandoned the use of hypnosis. Continuing to try and find out what caused hysteria, Freud became interested in self-analysis, where he would psychologically confront his own thoughts.

As a result of self-analysis Freud developed his psychoanalytic approach, in which he states that personality (the characteristics that make a person unique) is formed through specific stages of life, with different biological urges. He used the term Oedipus complex to describe a necessary stage of psychosexual development. In this stage a child's desire for his or her opposite sex parent, and jealousy towards his or her same sex parent, must be resolved by identifying with the same sex parent. For example, children will need to learn the difference between being boys or girls and to develop their own sexual identity. If children don't move through these stages, they will not move onto the next stage of development, and this may lead to physical or mental illnesses later in life.

Freud's claim that personality is achieved in a linear direction has been challenged over the years. We must now consider the influence and interaction that personality is shaped by both nature (genetics) and nurture (our environment and upbringing). These two factors merge together and have a huge bearing on our attitudes and traits. All these aspects affect how we think, feel, or behave in waking life and also influences our dreams.

Freud's structure of the human mind

It was Freud's task as an analyst to penetrate any hidden aspects of his patient's mind. He described the mind as an abstract entity containing three levels, and compared it to an iceberg consisting of the "conscious", the "preconscious", and the "unconscious".

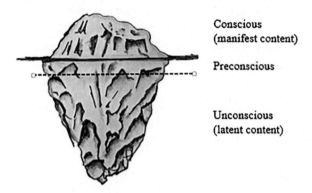

Conscious
(manifest content)

Preconscious

Unconscious
(latent content)

Figure 2.0 Freud's Iceberg Image of the Human Mind[3]

The conscious level sits just above the water. It's responsible for telling us what thoughts and feelings are available in our day-to-day interactions.

The second level is the preconscious which is underneath the water where we aren't always aware what is taking place. Information may be retrieved from this area, by recalling our memories and transferring this new information into our conscious minds.

The largest, lower level is the unconscious layer. There are two ways to look at what resides in this level. There can be experiences which were once conscious but are banished from our awareness because we would rather not remember them. They are often sexual, or murderous desires, and according to Freud, these need to be restrained in the unconscious. If they escape, they behave like a sleeping giant waiting to pounce, and may cause hysterical symptoms.

Another view is that there are mental processes which haven't yet been experienced, but are waiting to be discovered, such as a sixth sense. It's difficult to accept this view. If we aren't aware of these things, how can we be sure they really exist? However, I do believe there is a part of my mind where mental activity takes place, and of which I'm unaware. Whether it's a source of my immoral wishes, or something else I don't know, these processes are revealed to me when I experience an "aha" moment in my conscious awareness.

Freud's Dream Theory

Freud noticed his patients often referred to their hysteria as originating from their dreams. This observation suggests to Freud that dreams are 'the royal road to the unconscious'. Dreams take a short cut to the unconscious part of the patient's mind, enabling Freud to identify what's taking place. His ground-breaking work on dream theory is outlined in one publication, *The Interpretation of Dreams*[4] in which he uses many of his own dreams, and those of his mainly female patients to support his ideas. This book was initially met with opposition and ridicule, but later became one of the major influences in the development of understanding the human mind, and the meaning of dreams.

Manifest and latent dream content

Freud claims that dreams have two different levels. The first level consists of the details of the dream which we consciously remember when waking up and is referred to as the "manifest content". According to Freud, the manifest content is insignificant because it is a cunning disguise of the "true" thoughts of our dreams, known as the "latent content". The latent thoughts are unconscious and consist of wishes that are denied satisfaction. To keep the latent content at bay there is a censor which acts like a look-out, maintaining an imaginary boundary, to prevent these thoughts from gaining access to the conscious part of our minds. During sleep the night-time censor is not so vigilant, and can be fooled to allow unconscious material to move past the boundary line, and into our conscious minds.

The dream-work

As our dream moves towards a waking memory, these unacceptable dream thoughts transform into something more respectable through a process called the "dream-work". Freud maintains that dream-work is important because it has a dual function. Firstly, we can continue sleeping without being disturbed. Secondly, the dream-work changes the images to something less embarrassing, so they allow the expression of our hidden wishes during sleep. The two major operations of the dream-work which change our latent thoughts into the manifest content are known as "condensation" and "displacement". Dream symbols play a key role in this transformation.

Condensation

Condensation involves changing two or more parts from our latent content and transferring them to one object in our manifest dream.

Latent Content   Manifest Content

Figure 2.1 Dream-Work: Condensation[5]

In my dream about a former headmistress featured in Chapter 1 my latent thoughts may have been thinking about her in a derogatory manner, because she punished me for my part in the beret strike. I therefore change her into my grandfather in my manifest dream to disguise my revenge-seeking thoughts, and make my dream memory more presentable.

Displacement

Displacement replaces a latent dream image with a well-concealed allusion in our manifest content.

Latent Content   **Manifest Content**

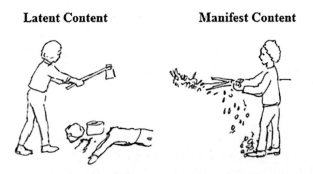

Figure 2.2 Dream-Work: Displacement[6]

If I dream of frenziedly cutting a hedge (the manifest content of my dream) then the latent content could be a more worrying desire – to chop off a lover's head, for example. The camouflage of the manifest content prevents me from feeling guilty about my murderous thoughts.

Freud emphasises that if we focus on the manifest content and deny the latent material, we may lose much of the important explanation of our dreams. I will return to illustrate these mental processes in more detail with one of my own dreams later in this chapter.

Free association

To help his patients to recognize their latent dream thoughts, Freud uses the technique of "free association" which enables them to identify and name their lustful or murderous thoughts. This method allows spontaneous thoughts to occur, and allows his patients to say whatever springs to mind about their dream images. To encourage this, patients would lay on a couch, and Freud would sit behind them where they couldn't see him. He then listened to their associations. For example, a patient's dream image of her husband may lead to the following verbal responses:

Husband → best friend → affair → hotel holiday and so forth.

The first association leads to a second, which leads to a third, and so forth until Freud decided when to stop. By doing this, he extracted chains of associations that went far beyond his patient's dream. To justify this, he argued that if he considered a patient's dream report as a whole, then his patient's mind will become blank. If, however, Freud fragments the dream into little pieces, his patient will then give Freud a series of associations to each piece. Freud used free association until he found an appropriate place to stop, but there is an uncertainty as to how he decided this point. Using this method from a single dream image, it's clear that he will end up with a large amount of information unrelated to the original dream.

Interpretation

When Freud gathered sufficient material to discuss the meaning of the dream he adopted a view of suspicion towards his patients, which was reminiscent of other professions at that time. His dream techniques were similar to that of the popular Sherlock Holmes character written by Author Conan Doyle, who was renowned for investigating clues for a "hidden" truth.

Both Freud and Conan Doyle had a background in logical reasoning, and applied interpretative methods of dissecting small details which provided an opportunity to open the door to a deeper reality.[7]

Freud practiced "interpretation", which today is a tool used by therapists to go beyond what a client has stated. It allows something to infiltrate from the unconscious to the conscious; by naming it in the moment, it makes the effort to break through to a conscious state. A "good" interpretation is either when it presents a new meaning for clients. Or alternatively, when unconscious thoughts make connections between current events to past events, and gives a new framework for the dilemma being presented. It can also promote awareness by stimulating more reality-based thoughts, feelings and behaviours, which in turn helps clients to recognise a new way of being.

Freud chose certain images from his patients' manifest dreams, and transformed them into different images, regarding them as the latent content. He used these expressions frequently, substituting them as hidden desires, and some of his well-known images are of a sexual nature. Elongated objects such as a pipe, a sword or a gun represent a penis, while a cave and other containers are considered to be vaginas. He then interpreted the meaning of his patient's new latent symbol, and most patients agreed his assumptions were right because of his superior knowledge. He claimed that by naming his patient's latent thoughts via his interpretations, the images lose their power, and his patients will be cured of their hysterical symptoms.

This activity denied his patients the opportunity to gain their own "insights" from their dreams. When I refer to insights in the context of dreaming, I mean when we have discovered a new understanding about ourselves. For this to happen and for it to have an impact, the insight needs to be experienced intellectually, for example as thoughts in our heads, alongside an emotion, such as a feeling in our hearts. One of the drawbacks of Freud's theory is that he only focuses on thoughts, which sometimes gives a spiritless understanding of a dream.

Freud's Dream of Irma's Injection

One of the most striking aspects of Freud's theory is his belief that all dreams are disguised, unfulfilled wishes. This revelation came to him through his analysis of his dream called "Irma's Injection". Irma, an eighteen-year-old patient, became his most famous dream figure when he analysed her for hysteria, but hadn't managed to cure her symptoms. He found she was uncooperative and didn't always take his advice. This resulted in the work being incomplete when they stopped the sessions so that she could go on holiday.

At this time Freud was staying at the Bellevue hotel in Vienna, getting ready for his wife's birthday. He received a visit from his own family doctor, Otto, who had been staying with Irma and her family at Irma's parents' country house. When Freud asked Otto how Irma was, Otto reported she was improving, but still displayed hysterical symptoms. Freud became annoyed by this response, as he rightly or wrongly attributed Otto's criticism to the fact that Irma's relatives didn't approve of him treating her. This disagreeable feeling that Freud encountered remained unclear for the rest of the evening, but he didn't discuss it with Otto.

That evening Freud wrote up Irma's case notes to give to another colleague, Dr M, for a second opinion. The next morning, he recorded his dream immediately upon waking. It was clear to him that it was connected to what he called the "day residue" (memories of people, objects and events from the preceding day).

The dream

Freud is hosting a party for his wife's birthday. He spots Irma, a patient of his who didn't take his advice of a "solution" (he does not say what the solution is) to cure her of her symptoms. He takes her to one side and reproaches her for not listening to him. Irma tells Freud that she is still in pain in her throat and abdomen, and feels like she is choking. He thinks he may have overlooked something, and takes her to the window where he examines her throat. When he proceeds to examine her mouth and nose he notices whitish, grey scabs on her turbinal bone. Freud calls Dr M over for a second opinion, who confirms Freud's suspicions that Irma has an infection, and not to worry as her body will rid itself of the poison. Freud remembers not long before Irma was feeling unwell, Otto gave her an injection of a propionic acid preparation. Freud thought injections of this type should not be given so freely, and probably Otto used a contaminated syringe.[8]

The next day Freud produced a twelve-page rigorous investigation, deconstructing the dream sentences layer by layer, like an archaeological dig. He free associates to each phase of the dream and links these associations to waking connections. I will only focus on the one aspect which gave Freud the "flash of light" he needed to discover the meaning of his dream.

When Freud is thinking about the injection that Otto gave Irma, he remembered that Otto told him about an incident when Otto was staying with Irma's family. Otto was called to a nearby hotel to give an injection to someone who suddenly felt unwell. This initial thought set off a chain reaction in Freud's subsequent thoughts. He noted Otto's injection to someone who was ill; which reminded Freud of a friend (Fleischl-Marxow) who died through using cocaine. Freud advised his friend to take the drug orally during his withdrawal of morphine, but he started injecting it immediately.

If we follow Freud's thinking it appears as: Otto gave Irma an injection (manifest content); → Otto gave someone else an injection; → a friend died because he didn't take Freud's advice (latent content). This example illustrates how making links from dream content to waking experience leads to early connections of the meaning of a dream. Freud's latter thought is from a previous memory relating to past events and is totally unrelated to the dream story. The dominant dream theme which instigated this link was an injection, both in the dream, and in Freud's waking life. The dream characters were important relationships professionally, and negligence would have been a great concern for Freud, particularly in light of an earlier death concerning Fleischl-Marxow.

Wish fulfilment

In waking life Otto annoyed Freud with his comments regarding Irma's incomplete recovery. This resulted in Freud's dream (manifest content) representing a state of affairs where he wanted to shift the blame onto poor Otto. The unsatisfied latent wish that he didn't want to be blamed for carrying out an unsafe procedure on Irma, becomes fulfilled (satisfied) when he is free of any responsibility of a mistaken medical diagnosis. In Freud's eyes it is Otto who administered the injection, probably with a dirty syringe, and caused Irma to have an infection.

★ ★ ★

Freud showed great insight into analysing his dream, and I believe he interpreted it truthfully according to his judgement at that time. He was so convinced by his theory that he wrote a letter to a colleague, Wilhelm Fliess, and asked him whether one day a marble tablet would be placed at the Bellevue, to acknowledge his achievement of revealing the secret of dreams. It would be many years before this accolade that he desperately wanted would become a reality.

Personalised Dream Interpretation: The Awards Ceremony

I will now further demonstrate Freud's theory with my dream below. His method has been adapted by me as with all the dream theories in this book, to make the stages more accessible for personalised dream analysis.

> There is a female person who resembles Cliff Richard standing on a stage in a crowded hall receiving an award. She wears bright red lipstick. What stands out are her high heels and black fur stole. When she receives the award, the audience applaud loudly. Cliff Richard then turned to the presenter. The presenter says she wants to nominate someone else for an award. At this point a rather insignificant female, shabbily dressed, resembling Muriel from the film *Muriel's Wedding*[9] comes onto the stage. When Muriel receives her award, there's very little applause and an embarrassing silence in the hall. Everyone feels sorry for her (1998).

I awoke with an anxious feeling from this dream. I will now follow Freud's way of thinking to change my manifest content into my underlying latent dream thoughts.

Split the manifest content into small phrases

Splitting the manifest content into small bite-size chunks, the segregation of the dream occurs where there is a scene shift, a change in dream character's behaviour, or the beginning of a new sentence or paragraph. My dream is now split into six separate sentences.

1. There is a female person who resembles Cliff Richard standing on a stage in a crowded hall receiving an award.

2. She wears bright red lipstick. What stands out are her high heels and black fur stole.

3. When she receives the award, the audience applaud loudly.

4.   Cliff Richard then turned to the presenter. The presenter says she wants to nominate someone else for an award.

5.   At this point a rather insignificant female, shabbily dressed, resembling Muriel from the film *Muriel's Wedding* comes onto the stage.

6.   When Muriel receives her award, there's very little applause and an embarrassing silence in the hall. Everyone feels sorry for her.

Free associate thoughts to the manifest phrases

This stage consists of the above phrases which are linked with any initial, corresponding thoughts. This process involves thinking about each phrase quickly, where I contemplated, 'What springs to mind when I think of this (relationship, object or event)?' My responses are shown as 1.A. to 6.A.

1. A.   When I thought about the Cliff Richard dream character I remembered in the days leading up to the dream that I watched two television programmes about music. The first was a documentary about Cliff Richard which highlighted his success and his many awards.

2. A.   The themes of success, music and awards reminded me of a second programme I had seen a few days earlier, in which a band called the Dixie Chicks[10] were appearing. In my dream the Cliff Richard character was wearing the same style of clothes as the lead singer of the Dixie Chicks.

3. A.   This phrase led into thoughts of my imminent BSc awards ceremony.

4. A.   I already thought of Cliff previously, so why did he need to reappear in my mind? Then I thought of the song title 'Wind Beneath My Wings',[11] recorded by country and western singer Gary Morris in 1983. It's a story about someone saying thank you to another person for doing something important in his/her life.

5. A.   In the dream everything was getting too serious, so I brought on Muriel to lighten things up. In waking life in the film, she was a hoot. However, humour didn't materialise in the dream as Muriel appears disadvantaged.

6. A.   The "Muriel" part of me in waking life didn't do very well at grammar school and no one applauded me during my time there.

My thoughts seem very incoherent after this stage, but already they show links to previous memorised experience.

Change the manifest phrases to the latent content

In this stage you need to get in touch with your latent content, which involves a deeper stage of thinking than the one you use to recognise your manifest content. I recommend you use "active reflection", which is a thought process that helps you to develop and integrate your new insights by reviewing your dreams carefully. This process can be compared to turning over a stone to see what the hidden side is like, or what is covered by it, so that nothing significant will be overlooked.[12]

When I applied this technique, I became aware of a sensation that I knew more knowledge was deep inside me, but it wouldn't float to the surface. I eventually got in touch with my latent content by focusing on each manifest phrase, and asking, 'What else do these new phrases remind me of?' My responses are 1.B. to 6.B.

1. B. The dream character of Cliff as both male and female represented my past relationships with men, and my relationship at the time of this dream with a woman.

2. B. I thought how the lead singer from the Dixie Chicks stood out from her two colleagues. Maybe I would like to "stand out" from the crowd.

3. B. The successful, professional part of me in waking life who was about to receive an award was represented by the Cliff dream character. The fur stole stood for the sash part of my graduation gown.

4. B. I immediately thought of my partner at that time who had supported me emotionally while I was trying to get through my degree.

5. B. Now the dream associations switched from male to female dream characters. I identified strongly with Muriel's troubled life, remembering the struggle financially, practically and academically to complete my degree.

6. B. I thought how I paid tribute to others by acknowledging the contributions of a former partner, family and peers towards my success. What I didn't do was to acknowledge my own efforts, by saying thank you to myself.

My manifest material has now taken a back seat and it's my latent content which is in the driving seat.

Free associate to the latent content

To free associate to my latent content I contemplated, 'What does each phrase tell me about myself?' I came up with the following thoughts 1.C. to 6. C.

1. C. I wonder if this dream is about me having a relationship with a woman?

2. C. I will like a little bit of fame when I receive my awards at Leeds Civic Town Hall.

3. C. Wearing the graduation gown will be a dream come true. It will make up for all the opportunities I missed to obtain a degree when I was younger.

4. C. I couldn't have done it without my partner's support.

5. C. The "Muriel" part of me is downplaying my success.

6. C. I am about to receive an award as a formal recognition of my first degree. I haven't acknowledged my hard work.

The meaning of the dream

When the latent themes are integrated they weave a dream conclusion which connects to current events. In waking life, I hadn't acknowledged my own contribution to obtaining my degree, and remained anxious about my forthcoming awards ceremony. There may have been some ambiguity regarding my choice to have a relationship with a woman who I loved at that time. However, I didn't see it as the main theme.

By applying Freud's techniques of free association, I gained some insights into the meaning of my dream. What I found helpful was to pick out an image which stood out in the manifest content, in the same way as Irma's injection was significant for Freud. The "stole" was important for me. It was the pinnacle of my understanding, and the hint of its role is there in my dream phrase, 'What stood out were her high heels and fur stole'. The dream awards represented my forthcoming awards ceremony, and the stole was a symbol for my graduation sash. This dream was quite simply telling me I should approach my ceremony in the spirit in which it was intended. As a result, I was able to receive my BSc award in a confident and elated state of mind.

A Freudian interpretation of the awards ceremony dream

As Freud claims that dreams hide their latent meaning through several mental processes, I believe he would have had a field day with my manifest reference to the ambiguous gender of Cliff Richard. I suspect that, according to him, my latent dream would include a man and a woman fighting each other, to determine which one of them I prefer sexually. I then morph them into a male–female image in the manifest dream, which absolves me of any responsibility to choose between them.

As an alternative, he may also propose that I change the Cliff Richard character, to make her more glamorous by giving her bright red lipstick, high heels and a black fur stole in my manifest dream. Changing her appearance to someone resembling a celebrity can be seen as disguising any sexual thoughts I may have been experiencing in my latent dream.

Freud might say I concoct all these troubling thoughts into a scene of a prestigious awards ceremony, to make the dream scenario more presentable. Although my Freudian interpretation is an assumption, I don't agree with Freud that this dream reflects the satisfaction of unconscious, perverse ideas. I approve of men and women having relationships with partners of the same sex, if they choose to do so. Also, I believe it's not up to anyone to dictate to another person who they should fall in love with.

★ ★ ★

Freud possessed exceptional literary skills and he could make even a far-fetched story seem true. I confess that I leave this chapter a modern-day Freudian groupie. He continued to live and work in Vienna as a psychiatrist until he and his family fled to England to escape the Nazi invasion. Freud died in London aged eighty-three from a lethal overdose of morphine, given to him by his physician to relieve his suffering from mouth and throat cancer.

He achieved the adulation he wanted, although his wish came true posthumously. There is now a plaque on the site of the Schloss Bellevue, a sanatorium where Freud worked as an assistant doctor. It was later turned into a hotel before becoming dilapidated and eventually demolished in the 1960s. The plaque commemorates one of the greatest thinkers of the twentieth century; it bears the words Freud said to Fleiss about his dream of Irma: In this house on July 24, 1895 the secret of dreams was revealed to Dr. Sigm. Freud.

## 3

Dreams Are Words of Wisdom from our Higher Selves

Carl Jung (1875-1961) is second only to Freud among the giants of contemporary dream interpretation. Most of the citations referred to in this chapter are from his autobiography *Memories, Dreams, Reflections*[1] written towards the end of his life. He was born in Kesswil, a village on the shores of Lake Constance in Switzerland. Jung's father was a pastor in the Swiss Reformed Church, and Jung described him as a kind, introverted, reliable man who encouraged a religious upbringing.

Jung perceived his mother differently, as he thought she had two personalities. She came from a wealthy Swiss family and believed in a spirit world, something that was a strong influence in the minds of people at that time. During the day, Jung's mother appeared to be a loving mother, but in the evening, she became entrenched in pagan beliefs. Jung heard strange noises coming from his mother's bedroom, and on one occasion, he saw her talking to herself. He likened his mother to a seer (one who can see spirits), but at the same time a strange animal – a priestess in a bear's cave.[2] I believe Jung was hallucinating as I think his description of his mother seems weird, but it's typical of the way in which he uses a "stream-of-consciousness" thinking to describe objects and people in his written work.

His mother's religious beliefs caused him to become a solitary child. He turned to his dogs as companions, and spent a lot of time walking with them, studying nature outdoors, where he was happy with his own thoughts. He described animals as having the trustworthiness that one might seek in close relationships. According to Jung, these traits are absent in some people, and this made him distrustful of others.[3]

Jung was persuaded by his mother's interest in the supernatural and this turned his attention to the occult. The general belief was at the time if souls survived death by leaving the physical body, they must continue somewhere in the world. Therefore, it should be possible to communicate with them. Some of Jung's relatives were engaging in table-turning, a type of séance where a group of people sit round a table, put their hands on the edge of it, ask questions, and wait for the spirits to communicate by moving the table.[4] He regularly attended these séances every Saturday night where a young girl cousin of fifteen acted as a medium.

On one occasion Jung heard tapping from the walls and the table, where he accepted the authenticity of these noises without question. These mysterious happenings were instrumental in turning his interest to the study of psychology and psychopathology. He made spiritualism the topic for his doctoral dissertation, but after receiving his doctoral award, he didn't know how to advance further in this field. Jung couldn't find anywhere to study spiritualism, as it was frowned upon and considered unscientific by the universities.

After he qualified as a doctor, Jung's family sent him to Basel University to specialize in surgery. While there, he came across a psychiatry publication by Richard von Krafft-Ebing who spoke of the importance of a psychiatrist feeling human towards his patients. This was in contrast to the poker-faced Freudian analysts who were dominating the psychology field during that time. After reading this book, Jung knew he wanted to be a psychiatrist.

Jung's fascination with medicine and spirituality inspired him to use both aspects of his personality which were developing in his work. He referred to personality number one as analytical, in which he had an appreciation of psychiatry from an objective point of view.

Personality number two, considered imaginative and mystical, was inclined to look at human nature from a subjective perspective. There is little doubt that Jung's second personality was considered to be a dark side of his character and was affected by his mother's split personality. This side of his personality enabled him to develop his own interests in philosophy, where he searched for meaning in his patients' histories.

Jung took up a post as an assistant at the Burghölzli Mental Hospital in Zurich, and later became a senior physician there. Here he worked with schizophrenic patients who experienced rigid delusional beliefs, along with visual, and auditory hallucinations. He became totally preoccupied in trying to work out the minds of his patients, believing they were not "mad" but that their dreams were full of valuable, creative meaning. Jung believed the visions and dreams experienced by his patients originated from a deeper level of the mind. He did not regard dreams as sneaky disguises attempting to conceal something.

Instead, he regarded the manifest content in a positive way, with dreams recognised as having power. Jung believed one of the functions of dreams is a language in which an individual's higher, wiser-self (the innermost self of our personalities) communicates an important message and reveals something previously out of reach. His view of dreams as compensating for something that is missing, suggests to me they are relevant to our state of mind at the time, rather than to something from the past.

Jung's House Dream

Some years later Jung met Freud, nineteen years his senior, who saw in Jung a protégé to act as an ally to promote his psychoanalytic theory. Their relationship was like that of a father and son, and Freud would often refer to Jung as his "crown prince", and a worthy successor to follow in his footsteps. However, there were radical differences in their theoretical perspectives.

The dream

During a boat trip to the United States with Freud, Jung began questioning the core of Freudian psychology. He had a dream that seemed to provide him with some of the answers as to how the human mind and personality were structured, and where dreams originated from. In current dream interpretation it's often assumed that a dream house can represent one's life or oneself, because a house is the dreamer's base. Jung's dream is as follows:

> Jung is in a house on the first floor resembling a comfortable salon. It's furnished elegantly in the style of the eighteenth century, and there are precious oil paintings hung on the walls. He begins to wonder about the rest of the house, and as he descends through the floors, the age of the building materialises into the past. On moving down the first staircase he reaches the ground floor which appears much darker and older. This level contains sixteenth-century medieval furnishings, and has a red brick floor. He comes upon a heavy door and when he opens it, he discovers a stone stairway leading down into a cellar. Descending further, he finds himself in a large vaulted room which looks very old. On examining the walls, he finds coatings of brick among the stone blocks, and fragments of brick in the mortar. He realises that the walls are dated from Roman times. He notices a ring

on top of one of the stone slabs and lifts it up, whereupon he sees a stairway of narrow stone steps leading down into the depths of a cave. The deeper he goes, the more remote and darker the setting becomes. As he ventures deep into the cave, he sees in the thick dust the remains of a prehistoric grave containing pottery, bones and two half-disintegrated skulls.[5]

The meaning of the dream

On awakening, Jung knew he had to find out the meaning of his dream and confided in Freud, looking for an answer. Freud repeatedly put pressure on Jung by asking him to identify a disguised wish in connection to the two skulls, and who the two skulls belonged to. Jung knew what Freud was trying to imply.

On the overnight train to Bremen, from where they had left for America, Jung had told Freud about the corpses that were perfectly preserved in the peat bogs in that area.[6] Freud became suspicious of Jung's interest in this topic, but Jung insisted on talking about them, until Freud eventually fainted. Freud was known to have fainting fits when he became anxious.

When Freud regained consciousness, he told Jung his morbid interest in the corpses represented a death wish towards him which caused him to faint.[7] Jung did have an idea what the dream meant, but, in awe of Freud's reputation, he knew if he opposed him it would lead to a quarrel. So, Jung told him a lie. He said that the dream was a death wish towards his sister-in-law and his wife Emma to whom he was newly married. This response put an end to the conversation, as Freud seemed relieved that Jung was not harbouring a death-wish against him.

Jung's structure of the human mind

When reflecting on his house dream, Jung writes in his autobiography that he is in 'an unfamiliar house', but then corrects this statement to say he also recognized it as 'his house'.[8] These comments tell of a split in his dream thinking, even at this early stage of exploring the dream.

As Jung moved down the levels of the house he realised he was descending the layers of his own soul. He discovered each successive layer connected him with an earlier time in man's history. Jung called the first floor of his dream "consciousness" as he became aware in the dream of what was going on. In waking life, he thought this level represented the most current period of his life because it appeared civilised. As a child, Jung lived in a dingy eighteenth-century parsonage and remembered there were two paintings in the dream which he recognized from early childhood. One is a copy of David and Goliath from the workshop of Guido Reni, and the other is a landscape of Basel dating from the nineteenth century. They inspired a lifelong interest in art which Jung later used in his dream work.

The fact that the next floor seems "darker" suggests to me Jung is dealing with the dark ages stretching from the medieval times back to the end of the Roman Empire. He named this floor the "unconscious" as it consisted of previously memorised experiences which were too fragile, had become irrelevant, or were too threatening for conscious awareness. Some dreams originate from this first level and are classified by Jung as "little dreams", because they are relatively insignificant.

Because there were no furnishings or artefacts in the Roman cellar I propose that Jung visualised this room as a non-materialistic one; and interestingly his analysis misses out this floor.

As Jung went deeper, the scene became darker. In the cave his first thinking towards a shared system of human functioning became illuminated in a "light bulb" moment. He considers this discovery his greatest achievement, and suggests that "big dreams" which have an impact on waking life, originate from this site. He calls this level the "collective unconscious".

Figure 3.0 Collective Unconscious[9]

According to Jung there are universal structures in the mind that reside in the collective unconscious which are common to all humans. He describes them as "archetypes". Although they are abstract they can be thought of as an inherited possibility to get us in touch with our feelings at a very deep level. This happens by transferring our symbolic dream imagery from figures acquainted with myths and folklore into something or somebody from our waking existence.

There is some evidence to support the view of archetypal imagery, such as similarities of themes in the mythologies of various cultures. Often in fairy stories, heroes such as kings and princes can outwit and slay evil dragons, and witches are shown as wicked. These stories are handed down through generations and do not change much with the passing of time.

It is my view that Jung's two skulls represent archetypal imagery. This is because he states that, on finding them located in the cave, he found the remains of the primitive man within himself.[10] Jung concludes the analysis of his dream as representing different aspects of the human mind which have evolved, and he carries this concept into his dream work.

Jung's Dream Theory

To obtain a psychological meaning from a patient's dream, Jung wanted to find out what previous waking experiences led to the images in the dream.

Amplification

To achieve this, he applied a procedure called "amplification" where he sat opposite his patients to discuss their dreams. In the same way that individuals amplify a sound by turning up the volume, amplification in a dream context increased the relevance of a dream image. Jung's criterion was to gather sufficient material to gain knowledge about a dream meaning, which involved looking at the dream as a whole and selecting an image for further discussion. He then explored his patient's dream image from an emotional point of view by helping them to recognise something they hadn't grasped before.

Emotions

Jung thought that if a new insight had an emotional feature, the patient was more likely to feel it at a greater depth with an increasing sense of connection. The words we use to describe our emotions affect how we feel during that moment. As a guide to assist readers, I include a list of the six universal primary emotions[11] along with similar meanings in brackets from a standard dictionary. I also incorporate the word "confused" which is not a primary emotion, but one which I think most of you will recognise when considering your dreams.

- Happiness (joy, excitement, satisfaction, optimism, contentment).

- Disgust (repulsion, hatred, dislike, loathing).

- Surprise (amazement, astonishment) or shock (jolt, bombshell).

- Anger (rage, annoyance, irritation, fury).

- Sadness (grief, unhappiness, misery, sorrow, anguish).

- Fear (anxiety, terror, dread, apprehension, worry, panic).

- Confused (disoriented, bewildered, muddled, perplexed).

There exists confusion and debate amongst psychologists as to whether a thought triggers a feeling, or if it's the other way around. For the purposes of dream interpretation, I feature "thoughts" as most dominant. I encourage readers to at least have an intellectual understanding of their dream, before branching out into exploring their emotions. In practice, Jung encouraged his patients to carefully record their dream reports and the interpretations they both reached. This is so that themes are identified through a series of dreams, and this exercise highlights the principal preoccupations of his patients at that time.

Personalised Dream Interpretation: The Black Dog

Using amplification with my dream "The Black Dog", I will illustrate Jung's techniques. The intensity of my fear whilst experiencing this dream caused me to wake up in a highly distressed state.

> I'm in a rundown car park parking my car. I have a small dog with me, not sure if it's Nora or Tina. She has to stay in the car park as I want to go into the building and it is too hot to leave her in the car. I'm worried as I didn't have a lead. Then I see my eldest daughter, Rachael, who hands me Tina's red lead. I put my dog on the lead and place her on a blanket at the side of the car. I ask Rachael to pay the

car park attendant the parking fee. I see a large black dog on a blanket in the next parking bay. It's growling at me and I'm fearful as it's not on a lead. I think it will harm my small dog and I become reluctant to go into the building (2011).

Draw the dream

Jung adopted drawings to portray his own dreams and in his work with patients. He thought it was a safe way for them to express their feelings. Even though the sensory mode of dreams is usually visual, it is traditional in modern sleep science to represent dreams with verbal reports. Representing our dream memories with illustrations can help to find a meaning from our dreams, when all other techniques have failed.

In this stage you are encouraged not to focus on artistic skills, but to illustrate a scene quickly and spontaneously to represent the main events shown in the dream. Where several scenarios appear please refer to my suggestions in Chapter 7 regarding my post-box dream.

Below is a drawing showing me as child-like, leading my dog Tina towards a building. There is also a black dog who's not in proportion to the rest of the dream, appearing as hostile and dangerous. It's growling menacingly at me as I approach the building to get past it.

Figure 3.1 Black Dog Dream[12]

Reflections from the drawing

This stage reveals any additional thoughts I discover by drawing the dream. I contemplated, how is the drawing different to my dream report? There are some inconsistencies. For example, I note I am alone and Rachael has disappeared from the dream. This difference is significant in the understanding of the dream, which I will return to later in this chapter.

Explore the images

The dream images to explore are down to personal choice, but generally we choose images that are important to us. I chose to associate my initial thoughts to each image and I asked myself, what does this image remind me of, and what are my thoughts and feelings that are evoked in response to it? This type of questioning will tease out memories that are close to the immediate proximity of the dream image. Where there are no obvious thoughts or emotions shown in the dream, I recommend that you imagine what they were during the dream. The images I chose are:

- Tina: In waking life Tina is my pet who is very sick with kidney disease. I feel sad that she doesn't have long to live.

- Nora: In my waking life Nora is a pet who previously died. I also feel sad when thinking about her.

- Rachael: Rachael was aged thirty-two at the time of this dream, but in the dream she features as a teenager.

- The building: The building is a representation although not identical of the veterinary practice I'd visited twice in the previous week with Tina. I am afraid that the building is a premonition of what's to come.

- The black dog: This dog is unknown to me, and at this stage I don't have a clue why it features in my dream.

Structure of amplification

In this stage I recommend that you chose an image to explore in more detail. There are three levels of amplification to explore an individual image, consisting of: personal, cultural and archetypal, and they are used in a hierarchical structure.

Personal association

I have picked the black dog to explore further as it's the image I know the least about. My model of amplification starts off as follows where I list spontaneous feelings that I associate with a black dog.

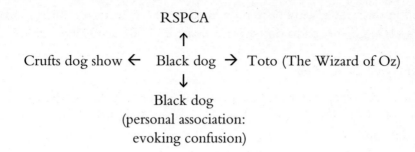

I donate regularly to the RSPCA, have seen *The Wizard of Oz* many times, and watch Crufts dog show every year. However, the meaning of the black dog in my dream still eludes me and is causing confusion. If personal associations do not strike a chord, then you should use the next level.

Cultural association

This level looks for a cultural association by asking how an outsider might describe the image to someone from another planet.[13] For instance, if I said, 'What is a book?' most people would respond with something like, 'A book contains many pages that you can read. It contains fiction or non-fiction content, and it's usually housed in a binder'. This type of questioning forces us to look at the image, visualise it and try to explain it succinctly.

When I asked myself what a black dog could mean to other people, I remembered in waking life two days earlier, that I watched a television documentary about Winston Churchill's depression, in which he called it his "black dog". His symbolic connection of a black dog and depression resonated with my own sadness around the choice I will inevitably make, by asking the vet to put Tina to sleep. My amplification model has now changed to:

Black dog

↓

Black dog (personal association evoking confusion)

↓

Winston Churchill (cultural association evoking sadness)

Through making a cultural association, my feelings of sadness have been highlighted. I knew that such a trip to the vets would involve a final visit with Tina and I could not bear the thought of that. Any reader who has been in the same ghastly position will empathise with my conflicting battle of grief, versus a need to do what is morally right for a trusting pet.

Archetypal association

If the cultural level fails to yield any meaning about the dream, then the final level consists of bringing in archetypal images which exist in the collective unconscious. Archetypes seemed to be the cornerstone of Jung's theory, and I believed there must be a valid reason why he included them in his model. Sue Masters, a friend and psychotherapist, consulted one of her highly researched dream books.[14] We looked up the significance of a black dog and found the meaning is traced back to a range of different origins.

Since the colour black is often used to symbolise grief and loss, it seems natural for black dogs to end up in mythology as precursors of death. In the folklores of the British Isles they are a night-time apparition associated with Hellhounds, described as huge, shaggy ghost-dogs with fiery eyes, and are a frequent theme in hauntings. They are unpredictable, hiding in the shadows, growling menacingly and waiting for an opportunity to ambush their intended victims.

When I add this archetypal image to my model, my thinking takes on a sinister meaning. The black dog in my dream is more exaggerated (as it was in the drawing), and changes to a huge, terrifying black dog. I am immediately reminded of the historical connection illustrated by Arthur Conan Doyle in his book *The Hound of the Baskervilles*.[15] The hound is inspired by a legend of a ghostly, big, black dog roaming Dartmoor. The main protagonist, Holmes, and his assistant Watson are out in the dead of night on the moors laying a trap to catch a killer. Suddenly, Holmes is frozen to the spot when he sees the profile of this ghastly dog which jumps out towards him.

> A hound it was, an enormous coal-black hound, but not so much a hound as mortal eyes have ever seen. Fire burst from its open mouth, its eyes glowed with a smouldering glare, its muzzles and hackles and dewlap were outlined in flickering flame. Never in the delirious dream of a disordered brain could anything more savage, more appalling, more hellish, be conceived than that dark form and savage face which broke upon us out of the wall of fog.[16]

The above account matches the visual image of the huge, black dog that I was reflecting on in waking life. I realised my fear was represented by walking past the black dog in my dream and taking my pet towards death. Thinking about the powerful description of the hound on the moors was made even worse when comparing it to my illustration. Rachael had gone, and I would have to face this unavoidable task by myself. My model of amplification now reads:

Black dog

↓

Black dog (personal association evoking confusion)

↓

Winston Churchill (cultural association evoking sadness)

↓

The Hound of the Baskervilles (archetypal association evoking fear)

My sadness, as experienced in the cultural level, has now been joined by fear. It's possible to find deeper levels of multiple meanings in a dream other than personal or cultural by using archetypal imagery. However, I suggest that you only look up archetypal symbols once you have exhausted your personal and cultural associations.

The meaning of the dream

The meaning of my dream is borne out of an accumulation of the feelings which are expressed in the various levels of amplification towards the dream image of the black dog.

- Personal association: thinking about a black dog generates confusion.

- Cultural association: a memory of Winston Churchill's black dog causes sadness.

- Archetypal association: a realisation of the meaning of Conan Doyle's big, black hound creates fear.

My dream is a metaphor for anticipatory grief for the feelings of sadness and fear that would accompany having a beloved dog put to sleep. This dream helped me to choose the right time, in consultation with the vets, for my dog to die. With deep regret my dream transpired into reality and, a few days later, Tina was peacefully put to sleep.

★ ★ ★

The only way I can join the dots up from my black dog dream, to Winston Churchill's depression, and then onto the archetypal image from *The Hound of the Baskervilles* is by using the collective unconscious. My dream was short, with straightforward imagery linked to current waking events, and this may have made an explanation easier to reach. This dream has not told me anything new.

However, the process of applying the collective unconscious has opened my eyes to be more optimistic about linking characters or objects symbolically, but only in the context of my own dreams. I recommend that readers who want to use archetypes to obtain a deeper meaning of their dream should shop around for a comprehensive, well-researched, symbolic dream book.

Jung's Dark Days

Jung lived most of his early adult life according to the characteristics of his objective first personality by focusing on establishing his career. By the time he reached the age of thirty-eight, his position changed, and he concentrated on establishing his number two personality by becoming interested in religion and spiritual mythology. Most of the academic world, including Freud, rejected his work, dismissing him as dabbling in the supernatural. This proved too much for Jung and he severed his relationship with Freud, which proved traumatic for both men. Jung knew that when he parted from Freud he would be spiralling into a lengthy uncertainty, and he experienced the aftermath as a horrible confrontation with his collective unconscious. It was during this time he saw visions and heard voices, just like his patients.[17]

Individuation

After the separation from Freud, Jung became isolated. He confronted the thoughts and feelings that lay in his collective unconscious, by using self-analysis which proved challenging as well as dangerous. He recorded many of these unconscious processes and they are featured in *The Red Book*,[18] in which he describes his difficult journey to overcome his own demons of fear and insecurity.

He began drawing small circles known as mandalas, meaning "magic circle" in Sanskrit. Every morning Jung drew imagery into these circles as a memory from his dreams. He studied the way in which the images changed daily, and they helped him navigate his developing state towards an inner self he called "individuation". Individuation is accomplished by exploring the world of our collective unconscious, making these thoughts and feelings conscious, resulting in an assimilation where a new balance is obtained, and making us feel "whole" again after being fragmented.[19]

This process may take years of studying our dreams; images will appear, disappear and reappear again and it's a slow growth. As a result of this gradual development, one can achieve a more stable personality, become less anxious and remain more contented[20] When Jung emerged from his self-imposed exile five years later he realised he had become wiser, and had achieved his true potential. This maturity was reflected in his forthcoming writings – before that time, his writing had consisted of a collection of rambling phrases, which made it difficult to understand his theories.

Personalised Dream Interpretation: Snow-Capped Mountains

As an alternative to amplification, Jung encouraged his patients to explore the significance of a dream symbol by engaging in a method he called "active imagination". I will now demonstrate this technique with the dream below called "The Snow-Capped Mountains".

> After I walk over the mountains I'm in a snowy village but don't know where. I need to go home but I can't remember the way back. I go into an old rickety building like a shanty town and ask three Mexican bandits for some money. They don't have any. Then two Norwegians offer to give me a lift back, but there are complications with that too. They only have two pairs of skis, so, I have to remain in the snow (2010).

Draw a mandala

Jung suggests it is helpful to draw a mandala after dreaming about inner turmoil.[21]

The mandala shows I encountered high levels of anxiety during the dream by holding my hands over my head in despair.

Figure 3.2 Mandala of the Snow-Capped Mountains[22]

Active imagination

The first step is to split the dream into four parts in the same way someone will outline a plot for writing a book. The first part introduces: the setting, the main characters and the situation; the next part is the emergence of the plot developing; the third part shows a significant conflict in the dream occurring; and the last part describes the outcome of the dream. Jung considered the outcome stage the most important component because it illustrates where our energy wants to go. It does this by showing us how to resolve an issue that is raised in the first part of the dream.

The next step is to enter a meditative state, focus on a particular dream image, and observe how the appearance of the image gradually changes. You need to interact with the image from a waking point of view to achieve a better understanding of its role in the dream. To do this you step into the dream picture, and if the dream image is a speaking figure or object, you speak directly to it. You listen to responses from the dream image, take seriously what it says, and respond.[23]

Once you have an awareness of the message from the dream image the waking life equivalent of the dream image is confronted. Using active imagination usually involves asking yourself how you relate to important others in your life. For instance, in the analysis of my dream I concentrated on the snow-capped mountains, and this led to me questioning a meaningful, long-term relationship. I closed my eyes, let my imagination flow free, and rewrote my dream as a short story.

Introduction: It's day-break and I am enjoying myself in a familiar waking location of snow- capped mountains. Later, as it's getting dark, I realise I want to go home. I walk on a little way and see some rickety old buildings. They look like the buildings in a spaghetti western which I watched two nights earlier. I go towards the buildings and enter. There I see three Mexican bandits and ask them to lend me some money, so I can get home. The largest of the bandits says they don't have any money.

Development of the plot: Suddenly, without warning, the shanty town and the Mexicans disappear, and they are replaced by two Norwegians. I ask them about helping me to get home. The taller one says, in English, that they would love to help me, but they only have two pairs of skis. They turn around and ski away from me. Seeing the Norwegians vanish into the distance reminds me about my disappearing childhood spent in Norway.

My memory recalls a white, snowy mountainous landscape which is idyllic. During the winter months my siblings and I went skiing in the resort of Holmenkollen. As a result, my early adolescent years felt very secure.

Conflict: There is now a contradiction about the dream-mountains, and they're not the backdrop for a carefree and safe activity. They have an aura of foreboding as the snow has disappeared from their branches. The mountains appear darker and their shadows dart in front of me, changing hurriedly. I feel a wall of doubt descending over me, and say to the mountains, 'Why have you changed from being somewhere I can have fun, to trying to trap me?' One of the mountains replies, 'We can't help you. Go away, and see if you can work out what to do about your relationship'. I rest on the ground for a while, and realise it is unsafe to remain as its getting dark. I follow in the ski tracks that the Norwegians left, and after a mile of plodding through the snow I start to give up walking.

Outcome: Suddenly I hear a voice shouting, 'We are here', and in the distance, I see the two Norwegians coming towards me with a sleigh pulled by huskies. I know my ordeal will soon be over.

★ ★ ★

By linking the outcome stage back to the opening scene, I realised the metaphorical impression of the snow-capped mountains enabled me to discover a profound meaning about my inner fears. At the time of this dream in waking life, I wanted to be back in the childlike frame of mind I experienced in Norway, where grown up responsibilities didn't exist. Instead I was in a conflict situation concerning a relationship with no sense of direction.

The meaning of the dream

The snow-capped mountains are symbolic of my mixed feelings of wanting to be alone, against wanting to be loved. I searched the symbol for mountains in Sue Masters' book and found that those which are breast-shaped and covered in snow are traditionally associated with a protective role.[24] I wanted the mountains to hold me as a mother will hold her child while I felt stuck, but the mountains changed and passed the responsibility back to me. I trod water in waking life for several years following this dream, but the difficulty concerning this relationship couldn't be resolved, and sadly, it ended in 2016.

★ ★ ★

Reading and writing about Jung has profoundly changed the way I explore and give meaning to my dreams. While writing this chapter I let my unconscious take the reins, and steer me into more creative interpretation methods. I consider Jung to have expanded my knowledge of that mysterious and awe-inspiring place he called the collective unconscious, which allowed me to feel my emotions at greater depth. I will remember him for his passion to discover the truth about oneself.

Although Jung travelled extensively throughout his career, he remained working in Zurich until he died at the age of eighty-five following a short illness. A few days before he died he had a final dream. He dreamt he saw a great round stone on a high plateau engraved with the words, "And this shall be a sign unto you of wholeness and oneness". The general consensus of opinion is that this dream represented Jung's work in this life as being complete. I suggest it also shows how he managed to reconcile his two separate personalities, previously shown as archetypal skulls, before he died.

4

Dreams Are Fragmented Holes in Our Personalities

Frederick Perls (1893–1970), better known as Fritz, a noted psychiatrist and psychotherapist born to a middle-class family just outside Berlin, didn't receive the same recognition as Freud and Jung. I believe he should have done, as his innovative approach of applying roleplay to interpret dreams was a refreshing change from Freudian techniques, which dominated the psychology field at that time.

As a young child, Perls remained happy until mid-adolescence when his relationship with his father deteriorated. He regularly witnessed his father's womanising ways and reluctance to support his family. This caused conflict between Perls' father and mother, and Perls grew to despise his father. His father constantly belittled him by saying, 'You're a piece of shit'. Because of this abuse, and after being top of his class at elementary school, he developed a wild streak. He played truant at secondary school, failed his exams and was expelled.[1] Perls' rebellious streak remained with him for the rest of his life, and was a major influence in the way he worked with future patients in his professional life.

Because he was unsuccessful in his exams, he was enrolled in a more progressive school, the Askanisches Gymnasium. The teachers were appreciative of Perls' independent streak and his interest in theatre productions. During his time there he met the director of the Deutsche Theatre, who encouraged Perls to play walk-on roles. When acting out these roles on stage, he learnt how individuals express their emotions through their body language. He enjoyed these performances which made his time at the Deutsche Theatre positive, enabling him to make up for the exams he had previously failed in. This early experience also served as a direct influence in the development of Perls' personality theory, and later his dream approach. He eventually became a one-man stage show, calling his dream group-work "circuses", and behaving towards his patients in a flamboyant, theatrical style.

Perls' family expected him to train in law and take after his distinguished uncle, but he chose medicine instead. During World War I, he trained in neuropsychiatry as a medical doctor, and, when qualified, he worked with soldiers with brain injuries. However, he was pulled towards Freudian theory, and a few years after getting his Doctorate he trained as a psychoanalyst at the University of Berlin and in Vienna.

Following the war and because he was Jewish, Perls and his family moved to the Netherlands for safety. A year later he moved to South Africa, and it was here he started a psychoanalytic training institute. He modified his Freudian beliefs when he encountered Freud at a conference, and it proved to be an unsatisfactory three-minute meeting. After the conference had finished, Perls went to Freud's room to introduce himself. Freud appeared in his doorway in a stand-offish way and didn't invite Perls in. The conversation ended abruptly when Perls mentioned to Freud that he had come all the way from South Africa for the conference, and Freud replied, 'When are you going back?' This rejection by the famous master of psychoanalysis was a rebuff that Perls didn't forget, and later in his career he resorted to publicly mocking Freudian dream theory.

More information about Perls can be found in his autobiography *In and Out of the Garbage Pail*[2] in which he writes "whatever wants to be written". He reports his mental ramblings in a humorous and candid way, and gives details of his many affairs with women and kissing men. This was a time when it was not taboo for analysts to sleep with their patients and Perls took advantage of this. He proudly labelled himself a "dirty old man" because of his ongoing sexual exploits.

Gestalt Therapy

World War II disrupted Perls' work when he joined the South African army as a psychiatrist. After the war, he and his family left South Africa, emigrated to New York and finally settled in Manhattan.

To put Perls' dream theory in context, it is necessary to discuss some of his "gestalt" therapy concepts (the nearest English equivalent word for "gestalt" is "whole"). This is because his theory of dreaming didn't originate from one of his own dreams, it was borne out of the back door of his gestalt approach to therapy. In Manhattan, Perls, his wife Laura, and Paul Goodman, a social critic and anarchist philosopher, founded their first gestalt institute and began travelling throughout the USA to conduct workshops and training. They published their book *Gestalt Therapy*[3] outlining a short-term treatment to help patients face things they were avoiding. This treatment was designed to enable patients to move forward into a more fulfilling life. In promoting his new theory, Perls emphasised that an individual's life should focus on free will and personal choices, as opposed to being governed by society's rules.

Perls' approach to the human mind

One of the major differences between Perls and Freud, is Perls' approach to the human mind. According to Perls, instead of a three-level structure, the mind can be viewed as having one level (the conscious mind), and is characterised in the diagram below.

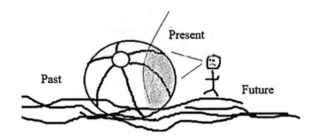

Figure 4.0 Man Visualising His Here-and-Now Experience[4]

The shaded part which the above character sees at any given time represents the part of the mind of which he or she is aware. This is as long as the character remains in what Perls calls, the "here-and-now" of current experience. The here-and-now is a process on an uninterrupted continuum. We cannot ignore our past, but worrying unduly about it, or what is going to happen in the future, can make us anxious. If we're anxious this prevents personal growth and leads us to a false existence, which means we are untrue to ourselves.

Perls' concept of phonies

Perls named people who he experienced as false "phonies" because they create bogus identities in order to gain acceptance from others. These types of individuals are recognisable by the way they communicate to others in a dishonest way. People who talk "chicken-shit" are those who use small talk and everyday conversation, like talking about the weather, or asking 'How are you?' This is instead of communicating what they really want to say. When people are chicken-shitters they don't feel vulnerable, as they don't reveal anything about themselves, which means they are relatively safe from being criticised by others.

Bull-shit is worse than chicken-shit because it includes responses of misleading rationalisations classed as lies; something Perls experienced from most of his patients. He suggests that everything his patients say before a "but" is bull-shit. For example, if I said, 'I would love you to landscape my garden, but I have already hired someone else', it could mean what I really wanted to say is, 'But I wouldn't hire you if you were the last gardener on earth'. Readers, please note I don't use the word "but" in this chapter for that reason.

The last category is elephant-shit. This is a form of speech known for its size and importance. People who use this type of response have grandiose plans, which means they avoid facing up to reality. For instance, I might say that when I win the lottery, I will give all my money to charity. It's highly unlikely that I will be that lucky, nevertheless, I may impress others with my intended generosity.

Perls claims that his patients using these "shit" types of speech were all phonies. As their analyst, his role was to bring to their attention when they are responding in a phony manner. For those readers who want to observe Perls in action, please see the extraordinary therapy session with his patient Gloria, on YouTube.[5] This session is an experiment to see how Gloria perceived three different therapists in 1965, and one of them was Perls. Throughout the video he challenges Gloria's misperceptions about herself, and pokes and prods her into admitting she is a phony. Despite his rude manner, Gloria chose him as the analyst who appeared the most helpful to her at that time. As Perls was part of the liberating "anything goes" movement in the 1960s that promoted existentialism (emphasising free will and individuality), he applied this unorthodox technique with most of his patients.

Perls' Dream Theory
Perls suggests these unhelpful traits of behaving as a phony manifest themselves through the most spontaneous of human behaviours – dreams.

From his point of view, the dream acts as a projection of rejected parts of our personalities. Projection in this context refers to how we transfer traits and emotions appearing as fragmented holes, which belong to ourselves, onto another person or object. It is safer to talk about one's vulnerability (including conflicts) in this way because our vulnerabilities are directed somewhere else, which means we don't have to deal with them.

Perls states that dreams can play a significant part by helping us to identify our holes, after our personalities have become fragmented. He claims we can recognise our holes by understanding our dreams with an investigative method introducing roleplay. This type of approach raises the potential to gain personal insights, because interpreting a dream in this way enables us to relive our dreams as though they are actually happening. Perls says that such insights usually concern internal conflicts about our own lives, or feelings about important others. Using roleplay techniques, conflicts materialise as the focus is on the connection to the emotional features of a dream, instead of describing the story or events which occur. It's possible that using this approach moves us away from the events which happen in our dreams, and into our imaginative experience.

The nightmare hounds

Perls believes that choosing two of the dream images, for example people or animals, and an object, may lead us to the message the dream is trying to tell us. Roleplaying involves us acting as the chosen images, and entering into a conversation with each other, until a conflict situation occurs. As the conflict emerges the holes appear, and are exhibited through two dream images that Perls calls "topdog" and "underdog" who are described in a masculine gender.

The basic characteristic of topdog is the part of our personalities that behaves in a parental or critical role. He makes unreasonable demands on our underdog by saying, 'You should, or shouldn't do this, or that'. Perls assumes we usually accept that topdog is right and we should do what he suggests, for instance, be better parents or get a better job. Topdog continues to demand perfection, and no matter how hard we try, there is no let-up from these constant requests from him. Over time these unrealistic expectations of ourselves are a damaging fantasy to our psychological well-being, because they start to become real and cause anxiety.

Perls claims that we create a worthy adversary who is in some ways more skilful than topdog. It's our underdog who appears less confident in our personalities, but he is also cunning. He tries to manipulate our topdog with phrases like, 'I can't do anything right. Poor me, I'm anxious'. Both strive to be in charge, and this ongoing conflict saps all our energy which should be used to create a productive life.

A dialogue between topdog and underdog is facilitated by adopting a two-chair method. While we are acting out different roles we need to switch seats throughout the conversation, to separate the dialogue between our two dogs. By repeatedly switching the chairs, the differences between the dogs become clearly emphasised, and a hostile situation naturally appears. We should also observe our tone of voice to see if it gets louder or becomes whiny as well as noticing our body language. Perls believes it's essential for us to play out each part of our topdog and underdog's personalities, so we can take responsibility for their actions, which might otherwise remain hidden.

The argument continues until we identify an impasse, a deadlock in the debate that leaves us feeling stuck. The impasse is freed up by reaching a new insight, which is usually when we realise what makes us stuck in the "warzone" situation. Once an insight is reached, the meaning of the conflict becomes clearer, and the two dogs make a truce to try to remove any anxiety.

Perls dream-group therapy

In the late sixties, Perls, aged seventy-six and working as a resident psychiatrist at the Esalen Institute in California, realised his dream therapy was more advantageous for his patients when he conducted his work in a group setting before an audience. Appearing before a crowd made his patients' more frustrated with their situation, because telling others increased their anxiety. They consequently became more in touch with what was causing their anxiety by naming it.

Perls facilitated his roleplay techniques by placing his patients in the "hot seat" in front of the general public. He made these public demonstrations entertaining by grilling his patients, and asking them embarrassing questions. He describes in his book *Gestalt Therapy Verbatim* a well-dressed psychologist took her place in the hot seat and said she wanted to fart. Perls told her to do so, and she did.[6] This is an example of the influence that Perls had over his patients.

Perls also queried his patients' body language with questions such as, 'What's your foot or hand saying?' to try and provoke an emotional response.

This technique is a way of exploring what is going on in his patients' minds, and he amazed his audiences with how much accurate information he retrieved by paying attention to their gestures and tone of voice. Many of his patients called him a "dahlink" and kissed him on his head as a mark of respect, after he had finished humiliating them in front of the crowd. The audience labelled his work a miracle cure, and many unorthodox therapists wanted to jump on the increasingly popular Fritz bandwagon. These group work demonstrations gave him guru status, and elevated his position even more amongst the general public.

Liz's Dream of Spiders and Tarantulas

Perls' techniques are illustrated with an example of his work,[7] which reports a live case study that took place at the Esalen Institute. He suggests that he and Liz, a patient, act out a dream conversation through roleplay in front of the group members, and an audience. He encourages Liz to describe the dream, whereupon she tells him that she dreams of tarantulas and spiders crawling on her. He suggests that a group member should participate to act as one of the spiders, but Liz doesn't want this to happen. So, he persuades Liz to talk to the spider, at which point she expresses an ambivalent response about whether the spider is ugly or not. With Perls' support, Liz eventually begins to use the image of the spider in a more positive way.

L: Spiders are necessary because they keep the insect, the flying insect population down (laughter). Spiders are fantastic because of the webs they can build.

P: Talk to the spider in terms of you. 'You are important because you …'

L: You are important because you keep the insect population down and you are important because you build beautiful webs … and you are important because you're alive.

P: Now change seats again … I would like you to try and let the spider return the appreciation.

L: You're important because you're a human being and there are fifty zillion of you and so what makes you so important (laughter)?

P: Now you notice already the hole in her personality – self-appreciation; lack of self-confidence. Other people have feelings of worthiness or something. She's got a hole …

Liz recognises through roleplay that acting as the spider, she doubts her self-beliefs. Perls instructs Liz to continue, and to direct any further conflicts onto the spider.

L: But it's up to her to fill the hole.

P: No, it's up to the spider.

L: What can the spider do about it?

P: Well, find out. Let the spider give her some appreciation …

L: Spiders can't think of anything.

P: The spider plays stupid.

L: No. She does some neat things but they aren't – she doesn't do them as well as almost anybody she can think of.

P: Are you by any chance suffering from the curse of perfectionism?

L: Oh! Yes (chuckles).

Liz identifies that she sets herself up to appear perfect, and starts to criticise the spider (herself) because the spider is stupid.

L: You should be able to do anything and everything and do it perfectly. You're a very capable person, you've got the native intelligence to do it and you're too lazy.

A conflict emerges between the opposing aspects of Liz's personality. She recognises she's adept at doing things, but is too idle.

P: Immediately you say something good about you, here comes the spider and shits on you. Do you see this?

L: Well, I think that's true.

P: Now we have got here the typical topdog, underdog situation. The topdog is always righteous – sometimes right, but not too often – and always righteous. And the underdog is willing to believe the topdog. Now the topdog is a judge, a bully. The underdog is usually very canny and controls the topdog with other means like 'manana', or 'You're right' or 'I try my best' or 'I tried so hard or 'I forgot things like that.' You know that gimmick?'

L: Oh yeah.

P: OK, now play the topdog–underdog game. The topdog sits here and the underdog sits there.

L: (as topdog) Why don't you ever do, anything perfectly?

L: (as underdog) Because I try to spread myself around, and I like to read.

L: (as topdog) Why do you like to read? To escape?

Perls picks up the conflict between the two aspects of Liz's personality and brings these to her attention.

P: What a mean topdog.

L: Yes, but it's also to improve my mind. I have to get some enjoyment out of life, besides being perfect.

P: Say this again. Say this again … Say this again … I dare you …

L: I have to get some enjoyment out of life besides being perfect.

P: This time I want to introduce a new element. Let the topdog go on talking to her, and I want each time to answer back 'fuck you' and see what happens.

L: (as underdog): You have a responsibility to yourself to fulfil yourself and get the most out of life and experience the most things and so on … Fuck you … But the topdog's right …

P: Say this to …

L: But you're right.

P: Who is it? Papa or Mama, or both together?

L: Grandma.

F: Grandma. So put Grandma in that chair …

Perls uses Liz's grandma as part of the dialogue (to replace topdog) to try and get Liz to see what her conflict is about.

L (speaking as Liz): Everything you say is true … but I don't want them …

P: I'd like to work on a hunch and I might be completely wrong. Say, 'Grandma, you're a spider …'

L (speaking as Liz): Grandma, you're a spider.

P: Change seats.

L (speaking as her Grandma/topdog): No I'm not dear. I just want what's best for you.

P: That is a stock phrase of the topdog as you probably recognise … Change seats again. Now what I would like you to do is close your eyes and enter yourself. What do you experience right now? Begin to feel something.

L: Feels like a spider.

P: What do you feel? What do you experience personally?

L: Do you mean physically?

P: Physically, emotionally, so far we have mostly think–think, talk–talk, things.

L: I feel like I'm – there is a spider sitting on me and I want to go do something.

P: What do you experience when the spider sits on you?

This challenge enables Liz to confess that she will scream if there is a spider sitting on top of her. Perls advises Liz that she should redirect this comment to her grandmother, but Liz can't do this as she feels too trapped to scream. Perls asks Liz if she is willing to enter a dialogue between a "good girl" where she does everything her grandmother wants her to, and a "bad girl" where she says such things as fuck you!

L: I'm a good girl and I use all my potentials to the greatest degree. All my – as my grandmother would say – God-given creative abilities, my God–given intelligence and appearance and whatever. And I'm just a very nice person and I get along with everybody. That's very nice for you but you're not gonna get any kicks out of life because I have a very good time and you can go fuck yourself (to Fritz). All I can think of is things that bad girls are supposed to have fun. But I don't …

P: Tell her that. Don't tell me.

L: See what you've done to me. You don't enjoy yourself and I don't enjoy myself and we wallow around in it. I can't be bad and you can't be good …

P: Now this is the point which we would call the impasse. This is where she's stuck.

Perls notices that Liz has difficulty in being the bad girl, and tries to "unstick" her.

P: May I have a private consultation with you? Your bad girl – is she really so bad?

L: I think other people would think so.

P: Ask them (the group).

Perls asks the group members to join in and feedback their observations to Liz. They suggest responses that makes the bad girl a good person such as: 'Your bad girl isn't bad enough', 'I think the bad girl's fine', and 'Her bad girl's pretty neat'. Perls gets the result he wants; the group are positive towards Liz's bad girl image. He then took the discovery of the impasse a stage further, by relating it to Liz's here-and-now experience of relating her dream to him.

P: Bad is what Grandmother disapproves of, and good is what Grandmother approves of. When Grandmother feels bad she calls you bad, and when Grandmother feels good she calls you good. She simply killed your soul, and the whole potential of your soul is missing. It's all mind.

L: My soul.

P: No, there is only mind. So there's a little bit of your potential used. I don't see any usage of your emotions, of your femininity, of your joy, joie de vivre. All that is wasteland so far. You are a good girl. And behind the good girl there is always the spiteful brat.[8]

Summary

By focusing on the dream from a feeling point of view, Perls gets Liz to look at her dream in a different way. He refers to Liz's lack of self-confidence as a hole which she can only fill by listening to the spider, and realising the spider represents the critical side (topdog and her grandmother) of her personality. It's undoubtedly a fact, that her grandmother had a huge influence in Liz's feelings of low self-worth, because of her expectations that Liz should always be a good girl. Liz gradually realises her spider dream was rooted in feelings of unworthiness, which caused her to reject some of the fun-loving side of herself.

Perls concludes this session by telling Liz she is torn between being a good girl to please her grandmother, and a bad girl where she wants to be herself. Despite his blunt manner, Liz seemed pleased with the end result, and thanked him for his help. Perls' final comment to Liz is, 'You notice that everything deals with the present. All talking about is out, all interpretation, all mind–fucking is discouraged'.[9] He couldn't resist having a pop at Freud and his technique of interpretation. Although Perls' methods didn't display much of the content of Liz's dream, they did reveal her insecurities at that particular time.

This case study demonstrates the dramatic results that Perls' skilful application could produce in a short space of time, without delving into his patient's unconscious mind. He was a proficient analyst and Liz's insights may not have materialised without his help. Unless a connection to waking life emerges between topdog and underdog, using roleplay techniques will be counterproductive. I recommend that readers who wish to use this technique keep an open mind, as the end result may not have a bearing on the original dream.

Personalised Dream Interpretation: Nellie the Elephant

I will now demonstrate further how to use Perls' approach by discussing one of my dreams I called "Nellie the Elephant"[10] which, on waking, left me feeling confused. I will show you, step-by-step, how to recognise my holes, and re-own them by listening to my dogs' conflicting personalities.

I take a small elephant called Nellie out of a kitchen. It's tied up in a long narrow kitchen which I don't recognise. Nora, my dog is there too. Then, I and Chrissy, my partner at the time, are in a bar ordering some food. We go outside into a big field with wooden tables and bench seats to wait for our food. This is the pub's beer garden. We sit down, and I look up and spot a man taking the elephant away from us. I become worried and speak to Chrissy about it. She says, 'It's good for the elephant to have a walk' (2012).

Rewrite the dream

The first stage is to write the dream out a second time and add any descriptions or information that spring to mind. The purpose of this task is to think beyond the dream story, and to try to identify any information which may be "sitting" underneath the dream. My extra information is shown in italics.

I take a small elephant called Nellie out of a kitchen. It's tied up in a long narrow kitchen which I don't recognise. Nora, my dog is there too. Then, I and Chrissy, my partner at the time, are in a bar ordering some food. We go outside into a big field with wooden tables and bench seats to wait for our food. We're in the pub's beer garden and we sit down. Then I look up and see *a scruffy man, who looks like the younger Steptoe character*[11] *leading the small elephant towards the dense woods. I become unnerved by this as he appears shifty, looking over his shoulder all the time. I wonder what he was going to do,* and say to Chrissy, *'I don't like the idea of that man taking the elephant away.' She tries to reassure me* by saying, 'It's good for the elephant to go for a walk' (2012).

Readers please note I have added three pieces of significant information. First, the dream man is compared to Harold from the sitcom *Steptoe and Son*, a television programme I watched in the early 1960s about a father and son rag-and-bone business. The programme focuses on the conflicting relationship between Albert Steptoe and Harold. Albert is foul-mouthed and has disgusting personal habits, which causes Harold to refer to him as "a dirty old man".

Harold is portrayed as a dodgy conman, wheeling and dealing in their business enterprises. But, he is also a decent man displaying traits of kindness which shows him as a lovable rogue. The man in the dream seems to have inherited both characteristics by stealing Nellie, but also appears kind by taking her into the woods, and leading her to freedom.

Secondly, there is now a theme of mistrust in the dream, as I wonder what he's going to do with Nellie. Thirdly, my mistrust is heightened even more when Chrissy disagrees with my dream-self by confirming it's good for Nellie to be taken for a walk.

Choose two dream images

In this second stage I chose two of the dream images which created an uncertainty. When I asked myself, 'What is the dream trying to tell me?' I came up with, 'I don't like the idea of that man taking the elephant away', versus, 'It's good for the elephant to have a walk'. I chose my dream-self to represent topdog, while Nellie will speak as underdog. They are the two consistent characters in both scenes, and while it may appear ridiculous that an elephant can speak, readers will soon witness the power of this approach. Since I sense there is a disagreement in the dream I commence the dialogue from the standpoint of a debate. I wrote my responses immediately as they occurred in my mind, switching chairs as the two images speak to each other. I also wrote down any bodily gestures or voice tone.

Identify the holes

To try and identify the holes, I need an evaluation of what's going on between my two dogs. This task is from a position of looking down at both dogs as though they belong to someone else, which helps me to observe what's happening as the exchange unfolds. My observations consist of my current thoughts and emotions, as I reflect on the dialogue "after" I have reported their conversation.

> S/topdog: Hey little Nellie, what are you doing in my kitchen (speaking in a bossy tone)?

> N/underdog: I'm not meant to be in here, take me out, I want to be free.

Already Nellie appears apologetic by saying she shouldn't be in the kitchen, and wants to disappear from the scene.

> S/topdog: You should stay here and be safe with me.

> N/underdog: I can't stay.

Nellie reiterates her earlier claim she wants to go.

> S/topdog: How come you're going off with that guy who looks like Harold from *Steptoe* to the woods (speaking angrily)?

> Steph changes her approach to try and scare Nellie into submitting.

> N/underdog: I have no say in the matter, he owns me now.

It works, as Nellie feels disempowered.

> S/topdog: But you don't have to go, you can break free from your lead.

> N/underdog: But I'm still small and he won't let me (speaking quietly).

Nellie shows Steph her vulnerability by being whiny to try and gain sympathy.

> S/topdog: I know that, and you should tell Harold.

> N/underdog: But Chrissy says it's OK for me to be on my own.

Nellie brings in Chrissy as an ally, and she is feeling strong enough to challenge Steph.

> S/topdog: It's not up to Chrissy where you go.

Steph tries to remain in control by implying it's not up to Chrissy, to have the final say.

> N/underdog: Perhaps Harold will set me free when we reach the woods.

Nellie looks for a way out, and clutches onto a positive side of Harold.

> S/topdog: He looks very sneaky – you shouldn't trust him.

> N/underdog: But I'm willing to give him a chance.

> > S/topdog: It's not a good idea. Say you don't want to go.

Steph is still in charge, contradicting Nellie's judgement.

Recognising the impasse

With Steph being more forceful by being protective and Nellie disagreeing, the battle commences.

> N/underdog: No, I want to try it. It will be better for me (speaking very quietly).

> S/topdog. I'm going to stop Harold from taking you away (wagging her finger and speaking very loudly).

The impasse is identified above when both dogs are stuck, because they cannot get their own way.

Freeing the impasse

The impasse is released when Nellie topples Steph from her superior role as she delivers her forceful phrase.

> N/underdog: You're making me neurotic. I don't give a shit. I will go (shouting back loudly).

Nellie is now topdog. It's usually the underdog who wins these battles, by arguing with topdog, and identifying the holes for the dreamer.

New insight

When an impasse is freed, this generally leads to increased insight. My insight is that I recognise the reasons for the underlying conflict between my two dogs. My dream-self is clearly worried about Nellie being led away by someone resembling Harold. This will leave her vulnerable as she is still a baby. How will she fend for herself in a dark and dangerous wood? However, Harold also appears kind by leading Nellie towards freedom.

The meaning of the dream

You are encouraged to create an understanding of the dream in terms of waking life experience, by asking what impasses occur which are creating anxiety. Using Perls techniques helped me to realise there were two opposite points of view that were troubling me, at the time this dream took place. In waking life, my free-spirited topdog wanted to be free from working. However, my cautious underdog regarded this as risky, as this would have taken me out of my financial comfort zone.

Some of you may wonder what the connection is between my dream and wanting to retire. There is no connection, but there is a similarity. Nellie informs me that it's alright to stop working by wanting to remain free. My dream shows that I projected an internal conflict onto my dream images. However, I am not convinced that feeling apprehensive is a fragmented part of my personality. I think apprehension is a normal reaction for someone who is contemplating giving up a secure job and leaping into the unknown. By listening to both sides of the argument the impasse is resolved by replacing it with an action stage.

What action if any, is required in waking life?

The action stage provides opportunities to consolidate everything that has been learnt and consider changes in one's life. As with any topdog–underdog situation, there must be a compromise to avoid ongoing anxiety. I gave careful thought as to how I could sort my squabbling dogs out. I came up with a solution to prematurely retire and six months later embarked on a creative writing course

★ ★ ★

Perls underwent surgery in Chicago, suffered heart failure and died there at the age of seventy-six. His reputation grew in later life because he learnt to cut through his patients' resistance very quickly, both face-to-face, and in group settings. He remained provocative and controversial in the way he worked with his patients, till the end. He had the reputation of being an authentic psychotherapist who encouraged his patients to develop their own personal identity, often from reliving their dreams.

I am reminded of the Gestalt prayer which epitomizes the work of Perls so well. He warns us to free ourselves from the continual disappointment we feel, when we fail to live up to the unrealistic expectations of the topdogs of our personalities:

I do my thing and you do your thing.

I am not in this world to live up to your expectations,

And you are not in this world to live up to mine.

You are you, and I am I,

And if by chance we find each other, it's beautiful.

If not, it can't be helped.[12]

5

Interpretation from a Series of Dreams
Increases Self-Knowledge

In this chapter I introduce you to a theory called "content analysis", which is a method of examining a series of dreams in a systematic way. Content analysis involves removing some of the content that makes up a dream and classifying it into: (1) the characters; (2) social interactions between ourselves and other characters; (3) objects that appear in the dream; (4) the settings; (5) the failures and successes we have; (6) the misfortunes and fortunes that happen to us and; (7) the explicit emotions felt by us when dreaming. These categories are compared to other dreams from the same period to show the frequency of similar dream content. When these details are interpreted, they help to determine our current preoccupations, which ultimately leads to a greater self-knowledge about ourselves, our relationships with others, and our environment.

Unlike other psychological theories in this book, which feature the interpretation of dreams as subjective, this method uses an objective view, as it's based solely on what appears in our dreams. By using an objective approach, we must disconnect ourselves from the emotions associated with the dream and interpret them from an outsider's point of view. When each dream is interpreted, the emotional features are re-integrated.

The first psychologist to study dream content systematically was Calvin Hall (1909–1985), who became disillusioned with the theories of psychoanalysts, as he thought their opinions were based on their patient's dreams, and not those of the general public. He classified the content of dreams from over several hundred dream reports, obtained from "normal" people. His publication *The Meaning of Dreams*[1] is the first of its kind to bring this type of dream interpretation within the scope of ordinary people.

Hall and Nordby's Content Analysis of Dreaming

Subsequently Hall, along with his colleague Vernon J. Nordby, published *The Individual and His Dreams*,[2] a guide for general readers to interpret their own series of dreams. In the following pages I have adapted their techniques to take into account my research into the meaning of dreams from a twenty-first century view. Hall and Nordby recommend categorising one hundred dreams to get started,[3] but I think that's too overwhelming. I therefore propose that comparing thirty dream reports is sufficient to get a consistent pattern of your lifestyle and current concerns.

Descriptions of the Classifications

Later in the chapter using my own dreams I illustrate how to classify the categories onto individual record cards. It's important to record the information exactly from the dream reports onto the cards except for the classification labelled "notes". This classification will be explained presently.

Characters

The "characters" consist of: individuals, a group of people, known animals, strangers, famous people, mythical figures, dead people and unknown animals. The dreamer isn't listed as a character in this classification. Hall and Nordby claim that most of the dream characters we use in our dreams are also intimately involved in our waking lives, and the frequency of their appearance reflects the extent of our positive or negative feelings towards that character.[4]

There are many strangers who appear in our dreams. Sometimes their role is significant by interacting with us, but occasionally they are just there in the background of the dream story. All figures who fit into this category must be examined to see what their role is, and whether they are a substitute for people in our waking lives.

A similar approach is needed for famous people such as actors, film stars, pop musicians and royalty figures who often appear in our dreams. Ask yourself why you have chosen this figure. The answer may lie in the name of the famous character, or in some quality which represents the character's role, or aspects of your own personality. When dreaming about mythical characters which are the result of folklore, or heroes, heroines and villains, it may be productive to explore whether they are perceived as good or bad, and their role in the dream.

It's important to identify our feelings towards any animals who appear in our dreams, as there is usually a message attached to their presence. Sometimes an animal can resemble a part of our personality, particularly where there is hidden conflict.

There are two stages to classifying our characters. Firstly, by listing on a sheet of paper each character and then counting the number of times that it appears. If a character appears more than once in a dream, it is listed once only. The second stage is illustrated under "My Characters" in the interpretation section later in the chapter. Characters can be classified as known persons versus strangers, or males versus females, or in groups, as shown in my character summary headings on my record cards.

Social interactions

The feelings that we experience for others can be determined by the number and the kind of social interactions we have in our dreams. The four most important and repeated interactions are described as aggression, friendliness, sexual and neutral.[5] In a series of dreams it's interesting to compare whether you have more aggressive, friendly, or sexual interactions, and whether you initiate the interaction, or another person begins the encounter.

An aggressive interaction includes physical assault (excluding sexual), threatening behaviour, angry feelings, annoyance, or irritation.[6] Friendliness stands for a deliberate act involving support, help, or kindness, towards another character.[7] Sexual interactions involve anything from having sexual fantasies about someone, to sexual intercourse.[8]

In some interactions we may engage in activities with other characters like talking or taking part in an activity in a factual way, where we don't display any sense of emotion. Hall and Nordby classify these interactions as "neutral".[9] They claim it's unnecessary to describe them, and they are therefore excluded from any interpretation.

Objects

There are many "objects" in content analysis and these are defined as something which has definite physical boundaries. Some of the objects that appear in dreams are there to tell the story and don't play a significant role.[10] Other objects are important and it's only by comparing a series of dreams that a significant meaning comes to light. The number of objects that occur in a series of dreams are many and will be different for each of you. Make a list of the objects that appear in your dreams, descending from the highest frequency to the lowest. I suggest in the final interpretation that you sift out the objects with a higher frequency, along with others that mean something to you.

The settings

The "settings" and where they take place are important and can make a difference to the interpretation of dreams. This is because dreams can sometimes be associated with a waking setting, even if it's not identical, but has a familiar feel. There are two types of classifications, indoors and outdoors. Indoor settings take place inside a building, for example a room, a hall, an office or a cinema. Outdoor settings are described as being outside such as on a street, the beach, on a train, or in a car, boat, or plane. Settings can also be classified as being familiar or unfamiliar, present or past, domestic or work and recreational.[11]

Failure and success

Some activities in dreams involve trying to think of a way to resolve a problem, and we may experience a "failure" or "success" for this event. If we don't achieve a goal, but try to succeed, then a success is recorded. I recommend that you compare the numbers of failures and successes. This will give you an indication of whether you are more failure-orientated, or more driven to achieve your goals, both in your dreams and in waking life.[12]

Misfortunes and good fortunes

Sometimes bad things happen to us in dreams which are not created by us, such as being lost or in danger. These types of mishaps are called "misfortunes". "Good fortunes" are good things that materialise by chance like finding money or winning a prize.

Emotions

"Emotions" are defined as specific while the dream takes place (not on reflection) and are the same experiences we encounter in waking life.[13] The emotional classifications are: anger, confusion, disgust, fear (including anxiety), happiness, sadness and surprise.

Notes

It's worth putting in this column any information which you feel may be relevant to the dream. These may consist of personal experiences, social events, familiar settings and any thoughts or feelings while reflecting on your dreams. The notes are used in the interpretation stage to determine if there is a link between your dreams and waking life experience. This category is something I have added to Hall sand Nordby's theory so that you may generate individual insight concerning each dream, before considering the meaning of your dreams collectively.

How to Classify a Series of Dreams

I aim to adapt Hall and Nordby's techniques using a series of twelve of my dreams dated 2017 because they are quite recent. I used a system of index cards measuring 210 x 148 mm (8.27 x 5.83 inches) as they are easier to handle and file, rather than a paper version. I found from past experience it's useful to code the dreams as they occur after writing them down, or recording them. As well as using the categories previously described the card indexes should contain the title and date of the dream, the series and the individual reference number. As already stated, the character summary can be changed to accommodate the number and type of characters you experience in your dreams.

Finally, the characters, objects, and emotions are listed individually as well as an accumulative score marked (x). This technique makes it easier to identify the total scores for each classification. The settings are preceded with a # to represent a familiar setting, or + to indicate an unfamiliar setting.

1/1. The Grim Reaper

It's getting dark and I'm trying to return home to Park Cottage before it gets dark. I stop at a petrol station and ask him when it will close. He says, 'Soon'. The street is dark and the lights in the house are off. I'm in a dark country lane, and a man passes by who has a hood over his face. He dresses in a black cloak and looks like the Grim Reaper. I'm afraid, but he just passes by.

Dream Series: 1/1		Dream Title: The Grim Reaper				Date: 2017	
Character Summary							
Strangers	**Famous People**	**Folklore**	**Unknown Animals**	**Children**	**Friends**	**Relatives**	**Known Animals**
1		1					
Social Interactions							
Character Type		**Aggression**		**Friendliness**		**Sexual**	
Objects		**Frequency**		**Objects**		**Frequency**	
Home		1		Hood		1	
Park Cottage		1		Face		1	
Street		1		Black Cloak		1	
Lights		1					
Settings							
Indoor				**Outdoor**			
				+ Outside			
				+ Petrol station			
				# Dark country lane			
Failure		**Success**		**Misfortune**		**Fortune**	
		I try to return home					
Emotions							
Anger	**Confusion**	**Disgust**	**Fear**	**Happiness**	**Sadness**	**Surprise**	
			Fear				
Notes: Park Cottage was a place I lived in between the ages of 19-21. The country lane resembled the track which led from the cottage to the main road. It had an eerie atmosphere.							

1/2. The wild boar

I'm in a large building on the ground floor. Some people are on the top, and then the building catches fire, and everyone runs out. The man fugitive is running outside, and an angry wild boar the size of a buffalo is also running loose. The fugitive shoots it, and he's let off his punishment for starting the fire. Someone wants to travel with him, but he says, 'No'.

Dream Series: 1/2	Dream Title: The Wild Boar					Date: 2017	
Character Summary							
Strangers	**Famous People**	**Folklore**	**Unknown Animals**	**Children**	**Friends**	**Relatives**	**Known Animals**
3 (4)			1				
Social Interactions							
Character Type		**Aggression**		**Friendliness**		**Sexual**	
A wild boar		Is running loose.					
The fugitive		He shoots the wild boar.					
Someone		Said, 'No' to the fugitive.					
Objects		**Frequency**		**Objects**		**Frequency**	
Large building		1		Fire		1	
Ground floor		1					
Settings							
Indoor				**Outdoor**			
+ Large Building				+ Outside			
Failure		**Success**		**Misfortune**		**Fortune**	
		The fugitive is let off his punishment					
Emotions							
Anger	**Confusion**	**Disgust**	**Fear**	**Happiness**	**Sadness**	**Surprise**	
1							
Notes: I was angry towards someone I knew at the time in waking life.							

1/3. The disappearing policeman

I wake up in a hostel on a ship. After I put my underwear on, I disembark and look for a station to return to Surrey. I book into a guest house and leave my bag there. I ask a young man where the nearest station is, and he points across the road and says, 'The trains aren't running because of the terrorist attacks'. I ask a policeman who's with some others how I can get home, and he replies he'll get me a lift. Daisy, my dog and the policeman's dog run down the road. I follow them and eventually Daisy returns. The policeman starts to walk away with his dog, and I question him again how I can return to my home. He continues walking and says, 'You'll have to sort it out by yourself'.

Dream Series: 1/3		Dream Title: The Disappearing Policeman				Date: 2017	
Character Summary							
Strangers	**Famous People**	**Folklore**	**Unknown Animals**	**Children**	**Friends**	**Relatives**	**Known Animals**
2 (6)			1 (2)				1
Social Interactions							
Character Type		**Aggression**		**Friendliness**		**Sexual**	
Young man				He points across the road and says, 'The trains aren't running because of the terrorist attacks'.			
Policeman		'You'll have to sort it out by yourself'.		He'll get me a lift.			
Objects		**Frequency**		**Objects**		**Frequency**	
Hostel		1		Guest house		1	
Ship		1		Bag		1	
Underwear		1		Trains		1	
Station		1		Home		1 (2)	
Settings							
Indoor				**Outdoor**			
+ Hostel, # on a ship, + guest house				+ The road			
Failure		**Success**		**Misfortune**		**Fortune**	
				I have to get home by myself.			
Emotions							
Anger	**Confusion**	**Disgust**	**Fear**	**Happiness**	**Sadness**	**Surprise**	

Notes: The policeman reminded me of someone I knew from the past, which brought back sad feelings. The ship resembled the cruiser, the *Braemar* in which I returned to Newcastle from Oslo during 1961

1/4. A stranger

I'm in a small room with some lesbians. I spot one who looks like a younger version of myself, and think, 'She looks nice. I'll go and ask her for a date'. Then the room starts to shake because it's under attack from a big group of animals. I become terrified and think, 'I need to get her out of here'.

Dream Series: 1/4		Dream Title: A stranger				Date: 2017	
Character Summary							
Strangers	**Famous People**	**Folklore**	**Unknown Animals**	**Children**	**Friends**	**Relatives**	**Known Animals**
2 (8)			1 (3)				
Social Interactions							
Character Type		**Aggression**		**Friendliness**		**Sexual**	
A younger version of myself				'I need to get her out of here'.		'She looks nice. I'll go and ask her for a date.'	
A big group of animals		Attacks the room.					
Objects		**Frequency**		**Objects**		**Frequency**	
Small room		1					
Settings							
Indoor				**Outdoor**			
+ A small room							
Failure		**Success**		**Misfortune**		**Fortune**	
Emotions							
Anger	**Confusion**	**Disgust**	**Fear**	**Happiness**	**Sadness**	**Surprise**	
			Terror (2)				

Notes: The animals resemble the ones featured in the television series *Zoo* (2016) who attack humans.

1/5. President Trump

I'm in a theatre but there's no one here, and then I get on the stage. President Trump arrives, pins me down on the stage and starts sexually assaulting me. I shout at him to stop, but he persists in carrying on, and tries to kiss me. I become panicky and yell at him, 'If you don't get off me, I'll tell the White House that you ruined my performance'.

Dream Series: 1/5		Dream Title: President Trump				Date: 2017	
Character Summary							
Strangers	**Famous People**	**Folklore**	**Unknown Animals**	**Children**	**Friends**	**Relatives**	**Known Animals**
	1						
Social Interactions							
Character Type		**Aggression**		**Friendliness**		**Sexual**	
President Trump						He sexually assaults me.	
Objects		**Frequency**		**Objects**		**Frequency**	
Theatre		1		Stage		1	
Settings							
Indoor				**Outdoor**			
+ A theatre							
Failure		**Success**		**Misfortune**		**Fortune**	
		I ask Trump to get off me.					
Emotions							
Anger	**Confusion**	**Disgust**	**Fear**	**Happiness**	**Sadness**	**Surprise**	
			Panic (3)				
Notes: In the news at the time there were reports of Trump allegedly sexually harassing several women.							

1/6. A visit to London

Barb, and I are in London. I want to go somewhere, so I give her the underground tickets and tell her I'll catch her up. I make my way to the station and get lost. I go to the information office at the nearest station, to try to get help to return to my home in York. My phone isn't working so someone lends me their phone, whereupon it transforms into my phone. I still can't get hold of Barb. Next, someone tells me that she heard on the news that I'm still missing. I try to call the police to come and collect me and to tell my mum I'm alright.

Dream Series: 1/6		Dream Title: A visit to London				Date: 2017	
Character Summary							
Strangers	**Famous People**	**Folklore**	**Unknown Animals**	**Children**	**Friends**	**Relatives**	**Known Animals**
3 (11)						2	
Social Interactions							
Character Type		**Aggression**		**Friendliness**		**Sexual**	
First someone				Lends me their phone.			
Second someone				Reports me as missing.			
My mum				Reports me missing.			
Objects		**Frequency**		**Objects**		**Frequency**	
Underground tickets		1		Home		1 (3)	
Information office		1		My phone		1	
Station		1 (2)		Stranger's phone		1	
Settings							
Indoor				**Outdoor**			
				# London			
Failure		**Success**		**Misfortune**		**Fortune**	
		I try to go home. I try to call the police.					
Emotions							
Anger	**Confusion**	**Disgust**	**Fear**	**Happiness**	**Sadness**	**Surprise**	
Notes: The setting is familiar from the time I was anxiously travelling through London a few weeks earlier with Barb.							

1/7. An African holiday

I'm on holiday in Spain with Barb, Chris, and John. I try to get something from the dining room to eat for breakfast. Because it's late, all that's left are cakes. A woman gets up from her table and says to me, 'Here's a cup of tea', but it tastes lukewarm. I go outside, and realise it's not a Spanish resort, more like a shanty town in Africa. I think, 'I'm not coming here again, it's not a bit like the Canaries'. I look for Barb and Chris and find them in the foyer of the hotel, sitting on the chairs waiting for me.

Dream Series: 1/7		Dream Title: An African holiday				Date: 2017	
Character Summary							
Strangers	**Famous People**	**Folklore**	**Unknown Animals**	**Children**	**Friends**	**Relatives**	**Known Animals**
1 (12)					1	2 (4)	
Social Interactions							
Character Type		**Aggression**		**Friendliness**		**Sexual**	
A woman				Says to me, 'Here's a cup of tea'.			
Objects		**Frequency**		**Objects**		**Frequency**	
Dining room		1		Foyer		1	
Cakes		1		Hotel		1	
Table		1		Chairs		1	
Cup of tea		1					
Settings							
Indoor				**Outdoor**			
# A dining room, # foyer of the hotel				+ African shanty town			
Failure		**Success**		**Misfortune**		**Fortune**	
		I try to get something to ear from the dining room. I find Barb and Chris in the foyer of the hotel.					
Emotions							
Anger	**Confusion**	**Disgust**	**Fear**	**Happiness**	**Sadness**	**Surprise**	
Notes: My response of, 'I'm not coming here again, it's not a bit like the Canaries', suggests I would rather be back in Gran Canaria.							

1/8. The missing station

I'm in a flat in London with Jim and another woman. We're getting ready to go to work and Jim shows me a gadget he built to make tea with. I ask him for a key, so I can return to the flat later, but he says, 'There's only one key'. When we are outside I ask him for directions to my place of work, but he disappears. I try to ask some passers-by the way to the nearest station, so I can return home. They gave me directions, but I still can't find the station.

Dream Series: 1/8		Dream Title: The missing station				Date: 2017	
Character Summary							
Strangers	**Famous People**	**Folklore**	**Unknown Animals**	**Children**	**Friends**	**Relatives**	**Known Animals**
2 (14)					1 (2)		
Social Interactions							
Character Type		**Aggression**		**Friendliness**		**Sexual**	
Passers-by				Gave me directions.			
Objects		**Frequency**		**Objects**		**Frequency**	
Flat		1		Key		1	
Gadget		1		Station		1 (3)	
Tea		1		Home		1 (4)	
Settings							
Indoor				**Outdoor**			
# A Flat				+ Outside, + London			
Failure		**Success**		**Misfortune**		**Fortune**	
				I still can't find the station.			
Emotions							
Anger	**Confusion**	**Disgust**	**Fear**	**Happiness**	**Sadness**	**Surprise**	
Notes: The previous evening I'd watched a programme called *Location, Location, Location* which featured the presenters trying to find a flat in London for three friends to buy. This dream reminded me of the time me and my siblings were evicted from a property during the 1960s for having loud parties.							

1/9. The secret service

I'm flying in a plane with some friends and we're sitting in the front row. The plane is cruising along an open road, and as it takes off we approach a crater with lots of fields alongside. We land on an RAF site and I ask someone where we are. Someone says, 'We're in Hull'. We make our way into an open-plan office, and I notice lots of people in RAF uniforms doing something secret on their computers.

Dream Series: 1/9		Dream Title: The secret service				Date: 2017		
Character Summary								
Strangers	**Famous People**	**Folklore**	**Unknown Animals**	**Children**	**Friends**	**Relatives**	**Known Animals**	
2 (16)					1 (3)			
Social Interactions								
Character Type		**Aggression**		**Friendliness**		**Sexual**		
Objects		**Frequency**		**Objects**		**Frequency**		
Plane		1		Fields		1		
Front row		1		Office		1		
Road		1		RAF uniforms		1		
Crater		1		Computers		1		
Settings								
Indoor				**Outdoor**				
# Open plan office				+ In a plane, # RAF site in Hull				
Failure		**Success**		**Misfortune**		**Fortune**		
Emotions								
Anger	**Confusion**	**Disgust**	**Fear**		**Happiness**	**Sadness**	**Surprise**	

Notes: The open-plan office resembled of one of the huts when I visited the Bletchley Park Museum. It was a happy time as the hut reminded me of my childhood days when my father was stationed at RAF Topcliffe in North Yorkshire.

1/10. On the beach

I'm at the bottom of a cliff on a beach with Sarah and my dog Daisy. I hoist Sarah and Daisy up the cliff, but it's only the height of a small room. When it's my turn, some of the footholds in the rock are crumbly. Eventually, I get to the top and go over to a group of young kids. I become anxious and say to one of them, 'You'd better not blow that smoke at my dog, or she'll get high'.

Dream Series: 1/10		Dream Title: On the beach				Date: 2017	
Character Summary							
Strangers	Famous People	Folklore	Unknown Animals	Children	Friends	Relatives	Known Animals
1 (17)				1			1 (2)
Social Interactions							
Character Type		Aggression		Friendliness		Sexual	
Myself		I warned a kid not to blow smoke at Daisy.		I warned a kid not to blow smoke at Daisy.			
Objects		Frequency		Objects		Frequency	
Cliff		1		Footholds		1	
Beach		1		Rock		1	
Small room		1		Smoke		1	
Settings							
Indoor				Outdoor			
				# Beach			
Failure		Success		Misfortune		Fortune	
Emotions							
Anger	Confusion	Disgust	Fear	Happiness	Sadness	Surprise	
			Anxious (4)				

Notes: The scene resembled the beack I was walking along with a friend in waking life the week before.

1/11. *Old friends*

I'm in a two-storey flat with Maralynn and Chris. We're getting ready to go to work. I ask Maralynn to leave our clothes from the wash basket out, and I'll wash them. As Nora hasn't been for a walk, I go to collect her but find her asleep on a pile of clothes. Then Maralynn's dad knocks on our door. After he climbs the first flight of stairs, he collapses because of his bad heart, but he tells me he's OK. I then ask Maralynn to take the other dog out before she leaves for work.

Dream Series: 1/11		Dream Title: Old friends					Date: 2017	
Character Summary								
Strangers	**Famous People**	**Folklore**	**Unknown Animals**	**Children**	**Friends**	**Relatives**	**Known Animals**	
			1 (4)		3 (6)		1 (3)	
Social Interactions								
Character Type		**Aggression**		**Friendliness**		**Sexual**		
Myself				I ask Maralynn to leave our washing out for me to wash it. I ask Maralynn to take the other dog out.				
Objects		**Frequency**		**Objects**		**Frequency**		
Two-storey flat		1		Door		1		
Clothes		1		Flight of stairs		1		
Wash basket		1		Bad heart		1		
Settings								
Indoor				**Outdoor**				
# Two storey flat								
Failure		**Success**		**Misfortune**		**Fortune**		
Emotions								
Anger	**Confusion**	**Disgust**	**Fear**	**Happiness**	**Sadness**	**Surprise**		
Notes: The flat is reminiscent of the flat I lived in with Maralynn and Chris in 1966.								

1/12. *The story*

I'm with Maralynn at the college. We're trying to write something like a scoop for a newspaper. I look for a person who can give us the information we need. I go all round the college, and up and down the escalators. I can't find the department, so I go to the reception but there's no one there. On the way back, I see a young girl who says she didn't want to do the course. Then I notice some paramedics who are removing sick people from the college. I become so upset that I can't write the story.

Dream Series: 1/12	Dream Title: The story					Date: 2017	
Character Summary							
Strangers	**Famous People**	**Folklore**	**Unknown Animals**	**Children**	**Friends**	**Relatives**	**Known Animals**
3 (20)					1 (7)		
Social Interactions							
Character Type		**Aggression**		**Friendliness**		**Sexual**	
Objects		**Frequency**		**Objects**		**Frequency**	
College		1		Department		1	
Scoop		1		Reception		1	
Newspaper		1		Story		1	
Escalators		1					
Settings							
Indoor				**Outdoor**			
# The college							
Failure		**Success**		**Misfortune**		**Fortune**	
I become so upset I can't write the story				I can't find the department.			
Emotions							
Anger	**Confusion**	**Disgust**	**Fear**	**Happiness**	**Sadness**	**Surprise**	
					Upset		
Notes: Te college reminded me of my last place of work. At the time I was considering going back to university to study more courses on creative writing.							

Interpreting the Dreams

Content analysis is interested in interpreting dreams individually and the whole series from a collective point of view. In Appendix E, you will find a list of questions which will help you to analyse your results.

My characters

My character summary reveals strangers (20), friends (7), relatives (4), unknown animals (4), known animals (3), children (1), famous people (1) and people from folklore (1). Out of a total of forty-one characters, after strangers, Barb, Maralynn, Chris, and Daisy show up twice, and they are followed by the remaining individual characters.

Approximately half my characters are strangers. Hall and Nordby claim that if many strangers appear in our dreams it may mean that we feel isolated from other people we know.[14] This situation may apply to some people, but I have two different views for the strangers who appear in my dreams.

Given that my dreaming mind produces illogical thoughts, it's not surprising that I select strangers to act as props, in the same way a film director may recruit extras to fill in the gaps when making a movie. Alternatively, a stranger can represent somebody from our waking lives. This is the case for the fugitive (1/2) that's battling with a part of me, the angry wild boar. I will explain presently the dynamic which is going on between the two of them.

There are eleven characters consisting of my friends, and relatives. Dreams of a sister Barb (1/6, 1/7), were indicative of the fact that in waking life I was travelling with her around the time of these dreams. On a separate journey to see two friends, Maralynn's presence (1/11, 1/12), and Chris's appearance (1/7, 1/11), confirms that dreams are inextricably linked to waking experiences. This is because I was dreaming about them shortly after my visits to see them. Dreams which show frequent major waking life characters suggest to me that they are important at the time, because they are included consecutively over a similar period.

There are three dreams (1/3, 1/10, 1/11) consisting of dogs which are known to me, and a further two (1/3, 1/11) featuring dogs which are unknown to me. I'm not surprised that dogs are included in my dreams as they're a great source of comfort to me, although I'm usually worrying about them.

There are two other examples of unknown animals. The angry, wild boar (1/2) replicates my dream-self who's disappeared, and she becomes symbolic of my anger towards someone I knew in waking life represented by the fugitive. By shaking a room, the violent animals (1/4) highlight my need to remove myself from an emotionally unstable situation, both in the dream and in waking life.

An individual from mythical folklore features in my dream of the Grim Reaper (1/1). Since he's renowned as a precursor of death, I realise the dream stirs up memories about the loss of my mum who died from cancer. President Trump (1/5) reminds me of someone I knew in waking life at the time, and I'll describe his role later in the chapter.

My social interactions

Aggression

I believe we are all capable of being aggressive under certain circumstances, usually towards other people. We express aggression in different ways, from feeling mildly irritated to wanting to attack someone. There's nothing wrong with being angry as it's a normal emotion, but I think when we are angry it shouldn't be bottled up. A more helpful approach is to communicate our feelings to the other person as this may dilute our angry feelings.

There are two examples of aggressive or unhelpful behaviour by myself and four by the dream characters or animals. My first aggressive act is by the angry wild boar (1/2) who represents a part of my personality that is running amok and appears hostile. Her dream behaviour goes against the response I previously suggested of communicating one's anger. As there wasn't an opportunity for this to happen, the only way to stop my anger is for the fugitive to shoot me (first aggressive interaction), which he does, but the exchange doesn't end there He silences me both in the dream, and in waking life experience. This was as well as refusing a request (second unhelpful interaction) from someone wanted to travel with him. Therefore, in this dream the fugitive came out on top.

Hall and Nordby report that feelings of ambivalence towards other characters are found in every dream series they investigated, particularly in women. They also say this type of experience is an offshoot carried over from Freud's Oedipus complex, in which young girls have both positive and negative feelings towards both parents, which continue into their adult lives.[15] This was true for my waking feelings towards a policeman (1/3) who reminded me of someone from my past. My ambivalence is identified by his inconsistent messages regarding helping me to return home and then changing his mind (third unhelpful interaction).

In dream (1/4) violent animals shake the room (fourth aggressive interaction) enough to make me want to rescue the female who looked like me.

There is a second example of an aggressive response by me (1/10) by me when I warn a kid not to blow smoke at Daisy.

Based on the aggressive or unhelpful interactions I don't appear as overly antagonistic. I believe my anger represented by the wild boar, and my warning for the kid not to blow smoke at Daisy, are justified for the events which take place in the dreams.

Friendliness

Some people are friendlier than others. There may be a very good reason why a person is unable to display an act of kindness to another individual or animal, and one of the ways in which this trait is revealed is through interpreting our dreams.

There is more evidence of friendliness than there are of aggressive interactions. Seven instances of friendliness by others, which are: a young man informs me that the trains are not running, and the policeman promises to get me a lift home (1/3); one considerate person lends me their phone, while a second person along with my mum reports me as missing (1/6); a kind woman offers me a cup of tea (1/7); and some helpful passers-by give me directions to the station (1/8).

There are four kind gestures initiated by myself: I need to rescue someone who looks like me from a room full of violent animals (1/4); I wish to protect Daisy from harmful smoke inhalation (I/10); and I ask Maralynn to leave our clothes out for me to wash them, and remind her to take Nora out for a walk (1/11).

Overall these interactions represent a balanced view of my personality and, at the risk of blowing my own trumpet, my family and close friends think I'm a helpful individual. Most of the time, I'm surrounded by people who have kind natures.

Sexual

Whether we think sex is the one and only pleasure in our lives, or less satisfying than reading a good book, it's at the core of our psychological make-up. Many of us dream about sex but it can present us with particular difficulties. Perhaps we are afraid to confront issues that are revealed in our dreams, or maybe we regard them as pornographic. An important component of understanding our sexual dreams is to listen to what they are trying to tell us.

There are sexual overtones in my dream (1/4) by declaring a stranger who looks nice, and that I want to date her. As this person resembles me facially, it could be seen as a form of vanity. I prefer to think that it felt safer to talk to someone who looked like me, rather than a complete "stranger". This is because, during the previous year a long-term relationship I was in led to failure. The image of Trump (1/5) symbolises a different scenario. On reflection, in this dream he represents a part of my personality that is warning me to avoid a sexual relationship with someone I knew in waking life. Since I don't find Trump or the waking character sexually attractive, this dream turned into one of my worst nightmares. Both dreams carry a message which informs me about the type of individuals I should or shouldn't have sexual encounters with.

Neutral

Neutral interactions are those which consist of talking or behaving with other characters that are not defined as aggressive, friendly, or sexual, but Hall and Nordby don't take these interactions into account. I will demonstrate from dream (1/9) how omitting these phrases loses the totality of the dream meaning.

- I'm flying in a plane with some friends.
- The plane is cruising along an open road and as it takes off, we approach a crater with lots of fields alongside.
- Next, we land at an RAF site, and I ask someone where we are.
- Someone says, 'We're in Hull.'
- We make our way into an open plan office, and there I notice lots of people in RAF uniforms, doing something secret on their computers.

With the absence of aggressive, friendly, or sexual interactions I become totally dependent on the objects, settings, my achievements, my emotional state and any links to waking experience to obtain a meaning. The above content raises important questions about the dream meaning. For instance, how come I'm traveling to an RAF site, and what will I do when I get there? Am I going to be enlisted as a spy, or is the trip a jolly day out?

You may think as I did, that the life has been sucked out of my dream. I haven't figured out, and nor have Hall and Nordby how to classify this type of data into a meaningful whole. This gap remains an important area for future development.

When thinking about this dream I realised it represented two things. Firstly, I had been contemplating returning to Bletchley Park Museum, as on my first trip I didn't get enough time to look at the codebreaking activities. This insight led to my second realisation about my father who was in the RAF, and the happy times when we lived at RAF Topcliffe in North Yorkshire, not too far from Hull. As interactions are not displayed in the dream report this left me feeling that the meaning was superficial. This dream highlights the importance of considering the dream characters interactions and behaviour to get an in-depth meaning.

My objects

I picked out the most frequent objects and then went back to read the dreams again, to see if there were any associative links, for example some of my dreams represent travel. The frequency of the word "station" in dreams (1/3), (1/6) and (1/8) denotes trains which represents my preferred way of getting from one place to another. I travelled extensively by train, both in my job as a former counsellor and in my private life.

Other objects such as hostel, ship, guest house, trains (1/3), underground tickets, information office (1/6), foyer, hotel (1/7), plane (1/9), cliff, and beach (1/10) are also associated with going on a journey. Since travelling is in my blood due to my father's military career I still travel as much as possible in waking life.

The word "home" featured in dreams (1/1), (1/3), (1/6) and (1/8) is significant, because in all these dreams I am trying to return home. In waking life, when I was a client my counsellor pointed out to me, 'You say the house when referring to your home, instead of my house'. By applying content analysis, I realise the search for a "real" home is continuous, as the twenty-five homes in which I resided have felt like transitory dwellings. Up to the age of seventeen my family moved to a different home every two years, from one RAF station to another. I've unconsciously kept that pattern up, by moving around the UK and changing houses in the same locality.

My settings

Outdoor versus indoor settings

This series of dreams revealed twelve of my dream settings were indoors, while the other eleven were outdoors. This is contrary to Hall and Norbury's claim that women usually dream of being in familiar indoor settings, such as their home, whereas men dream of being outdoors more frequently.[16] There are only two dreams (1/8, 1/11) which have domestic settings, which is characteristic of my present lifestyle, because I'm always on the move between different houses and places. Since their book reflects the attitudes of the 1970s, I believe I've moved on from the days of being a dutiful wife, whose sole occupation was to take care of the domestic chores.

My dream (1/11) relates to two friends from my past. To dream regularly about days which have gone implies that we live in the past,[17] and I often reminisce about old times. I put this experience down to my latter years weaving into my past more frequently, and as I age, such reflective thoughts are played out in my dreams.

If most dreams take place in a work setting, then our involvement is related to work issues.[18] In dreams (1/8, 1/11) there were references to going to work, but only in dream (1/12) was a specific setting identified. This reflects my waking situation as I'm now retired.

Familiar versus unfamiliar settings

Hall and Nordby claim that if a dreamer has numerous unfamiliar settings this suggests the dreamer feels alienated or lost.[19] Since only thirteen out of a total of twenty-three settings are unfamiliar, by their accounts I should feel reasonably grounded. I think it's more important to look at our familiar settings and how they may provide a link to our dreams. Included on the next page is a summary of my familiar settings.

Seven out of nine settings show the same emotions when reflecting upon the dream settings and comparing them to the original waking reminder. Therefore, the settings can be seen to influence my dream content with this set of dreams.

In two dreams my emotions are different. In the first dream (1/7) it reminds me of a happy holiday I had nine years prior with family and friends in Gran Canaria. This dream reflects a resort that's not up to scratch as it appears as a shanty town (normally acquainted with poverty), and the dining room has run out of decent things to eat. This dream provoked sad feelings

Table 5.0 Summary of Dream Settings

No	Setting	Reminder	Original emotions	Reflective emotions
1/1	Country lane	A cottage I resided in between 19–21.	Fear	Fear
1/3	A ship	The ship from Oslo to Newcastle.	Sadness	Sadness
1/6	London	Travelling in London with Barb.	Anxiety	Anxiety
1/7	Spain	A holiday in Gran Canaria.	Happiness	Sadness
1/8	A flat	A time I was evicted.	Anxious	Anxious
1/9	Open plan office	A visit to Bletchley Park Museum.	Happiness	Happiness
1/10	Beach	A beach I walked along with a friend.	Happiness	Anxiety
1/11	Two-story flat	A flat I resided in between 17–19 years.	Happiness	Happiness
1/12	College	York college, my last job as a counsellor	Anxiety	Anxiety

because there's a wish to have the same type of holiday I experienced in Gran Canaria.

The second dream (1/10) reminds me of when I went to stay with Maralynn where we experienced fun times. Perhaps I should have taken Daisy with me, to avoid the anxious feelings that appeared in the dream and in waking life by leaving her behind.

By using content analysis to interpret my dream settings I thought about them at a very deep level. I realise that identifying familiar locations is almost as important as identifying the role of the characters. We need to ask ourselves, are any of the settings familiar, what do they remind us of, and how are they associated to waking life experience.

My failures and successes

This category is about personal responsibility, but unfortunately as this series of dreams is relatively small I can only make tentative judgements. There is one failure in dream (1/12) where I become too upset to write the story. This dream coincided with my anxiety about being unable to continue to write this book. Shortly after, I consulted an editor, Alison Williams, who helped me to reorganise the original manuscript into a more accessible format for personalised dream interpretation. There are no failures by any of the other characters.

There is one incident of a success by a character other than myself. The fugitive (1/2) appears successful as he's exempt from his punishment for starting the fire because he shot the wild boar.

There are six examples of success which are the result of me trying to resolve a problem. In dream (1/1) I attempt to return home, and in dream (1/5) I endeavour to stop Trump from molesting me. In dream (1/6) I try to go home, and to call the police to tell my mum I'm alright. Dream (1/7) shows a further attempt by me to get something to eat, and eventually finding Barb and Chris in the foyer of a hotel.

As I have more instances of successes than failure, this mirrors my waking life experiences. Most people who know me, regard me as determined to succeed in things which are important to me, including getting this book finished.

My misfortunes and good fortune

There are no good fortunes shown in this series of dreams, which is line with Hall and Nordby's research where they claim that good fortunes are rare in dreams.

All my misfortunes aren't of my own doing: I have to go home by myself (1/3); I can't find the station (1/8); and I can't find the department (1/12). These experiences of trying to find something reveals that I was "adrift", which is how I felt some of the time in waking life.

My emotions

There is evidence of sadness where I become upset because I can't write the story (1/12), and an angry part of my personality is represented by the wild boar (1/2). I'm afraid of meeting the Grim Reaper (1/1) even in a dream, I'm terrified at the thought of saving a female stranger (myself) from violent animals (1/4), I become panic stricken at the way Trump is molesting me (1/5), and my anxiety entices me to tell a young person not to blow smoke at Daisy (1/10).

Half my dreams report an emotional state with fear and anxiety being the most dominant. They are natural responses to a real or perceived threat, with most anxious dreams originating from causes in our waking lives.[20] For example, in the dream where I am worrying about Daisy, it's highly improbable in waking life that I would encounter a group of young people who would blow smoke at her. This stems from an imagined thought, and the way to dispel it, or indeed any other dream which carries an unnecessary energy of anxiety, is to change what's happening in waking life. I take comfort from the fact that my negative experiences are revealed to me through my dreams. If they are expressed in this way, it gives me an opportunity to do something to alleviate any waking concerns.

Summary of Interpretations

For the final part of the interpretation I recommend you consider whether there is anything in your waking life you wish to change. Although my interpretations stem from a snapshot of dreams, they tend to indicate that I wasn't wholly satisfied with my waking life during that time. Because of my increased understanding, I now study my dreams more closely for mixed feelings towards another character. I question what this means by using Perls' topdog and underdog techniques and usually find a solution. The need to travel frequently is compatible with my nomadic existence, and I have continued to go on many journeys and take Daisy along where possible. I'm contemplating moving again and the next move will probably be my last. Consideration for future dreams will see if the dream events are linked to waking life experience of failures and successes and make appropriate changes. I will also examine dreams which contain misfortunes, particularly when it involves others, to see if there are similar events in my waking world that need my attention. Since last year, I have changed the quality of my life to live more in the present, and don't reminisce so often on the past. Using content analysis has helped me to build accurate profiles of my character and highlight issues that I wasn't previously aware of. Examining the resulting preoccupations, feelings, thoughts, and conflicts at the time my dream series occurred, has helped in making decisions about the future.

6

Dreams Are Random Brain Activity

During the late 1980s, J. Allan Hobson (b. 1933), psychiatrist and neuroscientist, emerged onto the dreaming scene, and created havoc amongst the psychological theorists at that time. He became something of a popular celebrity when he assembled together the nuts and bolts of modern dream science, as a result of his sleep experiments. These experiments resulted in a neurobiological theory of dreaming called "activation-synthesis".

He is widely considered to be the world's most important expert on sleep research, and is currently Professor of Psychiatry, Emeritus, at Harvard Medical School. His chapter does not include a psychological theory to interpret dreams in the same manner as the ones previously described. However, it contains important information regarding dream physiology, and it makes sense to hear what Hobson has to say.

As a young child, Hobson was influenced by the knowledge that was passed onto him by his father and his father's colleagues. They worked at the Hartford-Empire Company where they displayed creativity in engineering, by producing a range of different glass containers.[1] This resulted in Hobson discovering he had an ability that was useful in engineering, and by utilising his experimental traits, he thought his career would be profitable.[2] This characteristic, coupled with an interest in the natural world, propelled him towards the study of physiology and anatomy.

His mother had an equally large part in encouraging a curiosity about living things. She became an enthusiastic writer, and the young Hobson inherited her clinical, psychological brain.[3] It's therefore no wonder that he embarked on a scientific journey to attempt to bring together the two worlds of scientific discovery, and their corresponding meaning.

Hobson's curiosity in experiments began from a very young age. At the age of four he wanted to test how Santa Claus could come down a chimney by going up one himself. After pushing one hand up a neighbour's fireplace, he ended up covered in soot, and soon realised that stories of Santa Claus were a myth.[4] During this time he moved to a new house with his parents, adjacent to a wood, and up to the age of twelve he thought the wood was his laboratory. He spent a lot of time with his friends chopping down trees and building dens. This was in addition to capturing a range of small animals such as frogs and birds, and dismembering them for further investigation.[5]

His adolescent passion for experiments continued. At Wesleyan School he studied Freud and initially believed his views, but later decided Freud's theory was not scientifically sound as it wasn't the result of clinical investigation. By the time Hobson attended Harvard Medical School, he felt ready to challenge the established Freudian doctrine, and set out to change psychoanalysis with biological science. He began focusing on how the physical aspects of the brain neurons work, rather than concentrating on the mental processes of the mind, such as thoughts and consciousness.

One of the most debated questions in psychology and philosophy is, 'If the mind and brain are different, how do they interact?' There are two schools of philosophical thought that are still dancing around and have been doing so since Descartes' day. The argument is based on whether the mind and brain are separate entities. "Dualism" views them as separate, and Descartes adopted this view by claiming the mind is non-physical and is purely a thinking thing.

I know when I think, I experience a mental process in my head. I can't see this abstract thing I call my mind, but I know it's there, because it tells me what to do. Yet it does seem that the mind isn't the result of a magical happening which just arrives from nowhere. Most individuals of sound psychological functioning are aware that something quite powerful occurs within their thinking, and they relate their minds to a sense of self, and their personalities. Descartes recognised this, but he was unable to provide a rational explanation for the link between the mind and the brain.

The alternative view is "monism"– the belief that the mind and brain are the same thing. I regard my brain as a physical thing like my liver or my heart, and can't see how it instructs me what to do. Although I regard the mind and brain as two separate entities, I will use Hobson's definition of the brain to mean both the mind and brain simultaneously in this chapter, because that's how he describes them.

The Discovery of REM/NREM Sleep

Before explaining Hobson's theory, I will explain the phases of rapid eye movement (REM) sleep, in which he implemented as the foundation of his approach to dreaming. This phase of sleep was originally discovered by American researchers Aserinsky and Kleitman in 1953.[6] They noticed when studying babies who were asleep, that their eyes moved rapidly and jerkily under closed eyelids. In further studies with adults using electroencephalograph (EEG), electrical activity was measured during the same phase of sleep. The researchers observed that the brain proved active while the body remained still. They concluded that brain activity is associated with dreams, which led to a consensus that the phase of sleep known as REM is the physiological equivalent of dreaming.

At the beginning of sleep, we enter a phase known as hypnogogic. It's a process in which we are partly conscious and consists of rational waking cognition, and hallucinatory images that appear vividly and continue to change. We enter the first phase of sleep, and move through "ultradian" cycles, of approximately ninety minutes each cycle. The cycles comprise of different stages of non-rapid eye movement (NREM) and REM sleep.

NREM sleep

The first four phases are spent in NREM sleep. In stage one, our heart rate slows down, we begin to lose consciousness, but we can be quickly woken up. In stage two this sleep is deeper than in stage one, and we seem asleep but can still be woken up easily. In stage three, sleep is becoming deeper still, and we are unresponsive to external stimuli. About thirty minutes are spent in stage four – the deepest stage of sleep and by now, roughly one hour has elapsed since stage one began.

REM sleep

The cycle now reverses back through the earlier phases of three and two. After phase two, instead of re-entering stage one, a new phase five called REM comes into existence. In this phase it's even more difficult to wake us up. After fifteen minutes in REM sleep, another ultradian cycle begins, lasting about ninety minutes. However, with each ninety-minute cycle, the duration of REM sleep increases, and that of NREM sleep decreases. This means that NREM phases three and four reduces as the night continues, to make way for an increase in REM sleep.

If dreaming is more likely in the REM phase, this explains why dream recall may be at its most efficient for most of us waking from this phase at around 7 a.m. If we have between six and nine hours sleep a night, we spend approximately a total of 20–25 percent of sleep time in REM sleep. Just before we wake up we enter another phase of sleep called the hypnopompic phase, which leads us out of sleep, into consciousness, and into being awake.

Hobson's Activation–Synthesis Theory

Hobson and a colleague, Robert McCarley, published their activation-synthesis theory, which is described in detail in Hobson's main publication *The Dreaming Brain*.[7] I have only included the features which refer to the meaning of dreams from a psychological perspective.

After a series of sleep experiments, Hobson and McCarley formulated their ideas from three sources; (1) dream reports submitted by subjects in a sleep laboratory; (2) analysis of 256 dreams contained in a 1939 dream journal, written by a dreamer Hobson called the "Engine Man"; and (3) testing their theory using hundreds of Hobson's personal dreams for analysis.[8]

The results of his investigation produced a very large database with a great deal of common ground – all dreams contained the same formal features, which I will describe shortly. This gave credibility to Hobson's claim about the universal structure of dreams.

Hobson claims that dreams are a manifestation of random brain activity which occurs during REM sleep – and this is another important principle of his theory. His main disagreement with Freud stems from his theory that, because dreams occur during REM dreaming, they don't have a connection to mysterious messages that need to be decoded. Therefore, they have nothing to do with wish fulfilment.

Activation stage

Hobsons proposed that, in the activation stage while dreaming our area of the brainstem known as the pons creates electrical spikes that generate REM sleep. This then randomly stimulates areas of our brain above the brainstem called the forebrain, which is responsible for thoughts, sensations and feelings.

Synthesis stage

During the synthesis stage, as part of the forebrain activity, our sensory perceptions (the five senses) and motor information (what we do and where we go), are internally aroused and seek out anything in the memory system which remotely resembles this erratic output. When our forebrain encounters the bizarre array of random vision and other senses, it attempts to synthesise them into a coherent story. However, because the pontine spikes have been randomly stimulated by the forebrain, the end product is a narrative with misleading characteristics, leading to the experience we call dreaming.

Because of his controversial claims and his criticism of psychoanalytic theory, Hobson was labelled a "Freud-basher" by the many supportive Freudian psychoanalysts.[9] He strenuously denied this allegation,[10] but he gave Freud a run for his money, with his theory dominating the sleep research field for the latter part of the twenty-first century.

Formal Features of Dreaming

Hobson agreed with Jung that dreams are transparent and meaning and creativity are important to the dreaming experience, because they are integrated from images in our memory.[11] Meaning may not be present in the initial construction of dreams, but our personalities and current concerns may be reflected in the dream. Dreams can, therefore, be useful in understanding our psychological states, if we interpret how our dreams work at the physiological level. Hobson proposes that to understand a dream from a physiological position, the dream needs to be examined for its five formal features of: (1) amnesia; (2) sensory perception; (3) illogical thinking; (4) delusional beliefs; and (5) emotions, irrespective of their individual content.

Amnesia

A weak or no recall of dreams is experienced by many of us during the cancellation of memory during the brain-activated phases of sleep. Hobson claims that during this phase the instruction to "remember this" to our forebrain has been excluded. If our forebrain is not told to remember, then it will forget. As dreams are housed in a fragile short-term memory system, they can only be permanently stored if stimulation happens. This takes place when the dream is interrupted by us waking up. Then the perceptual and cognitive experience of the remembered dream is transferred to our long-term memory.[12]

Visual and motor sensory perceptions

Dreams are represented with vivid hallucinatory imagery consisting of "visual" sensory perceptions.[13] In a Zurich research programme, Strauch and Meier studied the descriptions of sensory perceptions from a bank of students' dreams. When they subdivided them into their different categories, the results show that in dreaming, individuals use the same five senses as in waking, to process information but to different degrees. Visual experience was the greatest with 56 percent, followed by hearing perceptions with 24.4 percent, then touch sensations at 19.1 percent, with taste and smell featuring hardly at all with 0.5 percent combined.[14]

It's not surprising that visual perceptions are dominant, as in waking life we rely heavily on what we see to provide us with information, and we usually communicate visual experiences in some detail regarding our dreams. Visual sensory perceptions are illustrated in my dream below which I called "The Headmistress".

> I'm in someone's lounge. I don't know why I'm there. Then we go to a school fete, and we sit in the cellar of the school in Carlisle, and there is a small group. I ask the headmistress if it's a fashion show. The headmistress is in our group; she seems very informal. Then we watch a film they made to publicise the school. The headmistress is rolling on the grass laughing, looking like the headmistress in the *St Trinian's*[15] films. I look up at the scaffolding holding up the school, and someone says the school is very old, and they can't dismantle the scaffolding (1998).

Despite the scene having an illogical story, which could be classed as hallucinatory from someone who appears quite "mad", the scenes are described very clearly.

We also construct hallucinatory "motor movement" (what we do in dreams)[16] which plays a large part in dreams and accompanies the visual images. In the above dream I move through the dream as it changes, although I don't show how. It could appear that I have been placed in the different scenes by an invisible hand, starting off with my dream-self appearing in a lounge, then inside a cellar and finally being outside. On reflecting of this dream it made perfect sense to me. The day before, in waking life, I had contemplated visiting some old friends from my former grammar school.

Illogical thinking

Hobson states that "illogical thinking" is the result of changing physiological aspects that take place during sleep. Most dreams are disorganised with irrational thinking taking place, and aspects such as places, time, and people change suddenly without notice.[17] This results in unreliable or implausible combinations of characters and events within the dream experience.

Thinking in dreams is different to the thought processes which happen when we're awake. Strauch and Meier found, when analysing students' descriptions of their dreams, 42.7 percent were thoughts, making thinking an essential part of their dreams.[18] The researchers didn't find evidence of the students contemplating complicated problems, tackling difficult relationships, or asking questions logically from different viewpoints.[19] The students appear to accept situations of the moment, not asking what's happened before an event, or what will occur later.

An example of a dream where I haven't thought things through, is shown in the following dream, "A Baby Boy" which, on waking, left me feeling confused.

> Someone knocks on the door and I'm given a baby boy to look after. He is wearing a blue all-in-one suit and is about a year old. He's sick, so I rush next door to the doctors, but they don't take me seriously. One of the doctors has a quick look and says he's OK. When I get home, I try to find out which agency has delivered him. I don't want him as I want to get on with my thesis. The baby starts to walk even though he is very young. I feel relieved, and then I'm on the phone to my academic supervisor, telling him what has happened (2009).

The dream starts off with my dream-self deciding to seek medical help for a sick baby. The events change when I attempt to banish him away, so I can attend to the more important business of completing my thesis. That fails, and it's only when he goes away of his own accord that I feel a sense of relief. By telling my supervisor what happened, I enlisted him as an ally to approve of my abdication of responsibility for taking care of a young boy.

What is unknown to me while reflecting on this dream, is why my dreaming mind chose a baby to portray an unwanted duty, as opposed to more appropriate events such as pressure from my clinical work. My thought processes are mainly single-minded. They exclude information about the someone who knocked on the door, how I'm chosen to look after a baby, why I accepted the doctor's opinion of the baby being OK when he is clearly sick, and the reason why an academic supervisor is involved in a domestic situation. If this incident had happened in waking life, many more questions would be asked, leading to fuller explanations. Answers to these questions will feature in Chapter 7 (under dream thoughts and links to waking experience).

Lucid dreaming

There exists another thought process which Hobson doesn't mention, but because of its popularity I will give a brief outline – it's called "lucid dreaming". During this state of dreaming in which we are consciously aware we are dreaming, we may be able to have some control over characters, their behaviour and the context of the dream. My following dream, which I called "Morrisons", illustrates some lucid features, and includes a reality which could be possible in waking life. I felt slightly apprehensive when waking up from this dream.

> I'm with my daughters Rachael and Sarah and some other people in an open-top car. We drive off to a supermarket to get some food for Sarah. She tells me she can't get the meat from Morrisons as its too expensive, and she doesn't have any tokens. I say to her, 'Tell me what you want, and I'll get it' (2014).

I used my dream thoughts in a similar way to waking life, by driving the story forward to obtain a solution for Sarah's lack of finances. Being helpful about money was a legitimate mode of action, given Sarah was coming to the end of her student grants. It's clear to see that I'm attempting a "mum" type favour to assist her, by offering to pay for her shopping.

Morrisons is a shop I regularly use in waking life. Other than my two daughters, I didn't know the other people in the car. In waking life, I did recognise the car. It resembled an open-top convertible I was swanning around in London during the mid-1960s. I believe this part of the dream to be a confused selection from my memory banks, and nothing more than a vehicle to transport us to Morrisons. My dreaming mind needed a car and it chose a red convertible from the sixties, rather than the old Nissan that I currently have. Perhaps I would rather be eighteen again, and having a few drinks in the West End of London. Dream logic with such obvious clarity is very rare in my personal experience, and I can't offer a rational explanation as to why this dream contains lucid features, and others don't.

Lucid dreams are much easier to understand due to a reduction in illogical events, and I can see why some of us would like to have a repertoire of tools to encourage this experience. The wish to open our minds to a higher plane of awareness is a current trend, and there exists much literature on how to develop techniques to achieve this. One of the most helpful books regarding lucid dreaming is a guide by Stephen LaBerge called *Exploring the World of Lucid Dreams*.[20] For myself, I much prefer to be battling my wits against the more complex features in dreaming, which prove more challenging. There is considerable benefit in knowing I have uncovered an understanding which was previously out of reach.

Delusional beliefs

Following on from dream thoughts, according to Hobson our dreaming brains accept the "delusional beliefs" that are featured in our dreams.[21] This is due to the strong perceptions and emotional states that happen during dreaming, no matter how bizarre they may be. Some delusional features will be demonstrated with my own dream later in this chapter.

Emotions

Hobson acknowledges the increased activity of the limbic system, which is a part of the brain that produces intense "emotions" such as fear, anxiety and surprise, during REM sleep.[22] He claims that discovering the underlying emotional theme is the key to unlocking the meaning of a dream. This category is one of the most helpful features of his model, and it's particularly significant as the previous models don't have a direct intervention to facilitate emotion.

In contradiction to Hobson's view, Strauch and Meier confirm considerably less evidence of emotional dream experience with 8.9 percent compared to thoughts and sensory perceptions.[23] This is surprising, as in waking life we spend a lot of time feeling things which have a huge impact on our general well-being and behaviour.

The researchers didn't obtain data for emotional content from the subjects' dream reports, but instead asked the subjects once they were awake how they felt during the dream. Overall, subjects showed the same emotional response that one would have in waking life facing a similar situation. However, some reports lacked the emotional involvement that would have been part of the same experience while awake. As a significant number of dreams didn't report emotions, the researchers claim their results contradict the view that emotions are critical to the dream events.[24]

I disagree with Strauch and Meier, and I believe Hobson is correct that emotions form a critical link to understanding a dream. A factor which may contribute to a lack of emotion is the process of dream recall. On waking, we report dreams from a distance, as though our dreams belong to someone else, and during this transient phase our emotions may be hard to detect.

While emotions are frequently absent in dreams, it doesn't mean they don't exist. In waking life, many of us find it difficult to express our emotions, and I see no reason why this shouldn't be the same in the dream state. I believe some of Strauch and Meier's subjects will fall into this category, particularly as the researchers chose to ask the participants how they felt after the dream. Based on this contradiction, it's my view that we should evaluate our emotions from the dream events, and on reflections from waking.

Personalised Formal Analysis of the Money Dream

Hobson claims that by using his formal characteristics to interpret our dreams, this can help us to recognise their underlying conflicts and emotion. I have modified Hobson's guidelines[25] to make the questions relevant for personalised interpretation. I awoke from this dream with high levels of anxiety and feeling confused.

> I'm with my niece Chloe and some other people trying to get ready to avoid a war. I have some money (dollars) and I go to a department store in America to buy dark green wallpaper. I leave the money in the wallpaper section of the store, go for a coffee and realise I've lost a lot of money. I find a plastic bag with one piece of paper money left. I go to a hatch and ask to speak to a security guard who looks a bit like me and I explain the story. I tell him a tramp has taken my money, and he replies he will get the tramp and get my money back (2002).

I have discarded the first two categories of amnesia and sensory perceptions. Amnesia is self-explanatory, and because we may not remember all of a dream, this realisation doesn't add anything to the psychological meaning of a dream. The visual sensory perception is described adequately in the dream report. Any motor perception that appears as hallucinatory will be teased out by examining my illogical thinking and delusional beliefs.

Illogical thoughts

Places

The scenes jump from one to another without a meaningful link. Although I visited America twelve years before I had this dream in waking life, I didn't go to a wallpaper shop. In the dream, if I ended up buying the wallpaper in America it's unclear how I got there. Perhaps I am already there, and have magical powers to beam myself up as characters do in science fiction novels.

Time

Chloe, my niece, is shown at the age of eleven, which is twelve years younger than she was in waking life at the time of this dream. I am shown at my current age at that time, of fifty-four.

People

The security guard resembles me, but I describe him in the masculine sense. Is this a throwback to my ambiguous sexuality mentioned in my awards ceremony dream? Or, is it that I believe he'll get the scoundrel who stole my money more easily by dressing as a man.

Delusions

I mention that my dream-self, Chloe and the others are trying to get ready to avoid a war. However, there are no details as to why we are stuck there, or how we behave to prevent it. Am I and the others trying to protect ourselves from an alien invasion, or are we faced with World War III, even though there is nothing happening around us to suggest that a war is imminent?

Chloe, the others and the security guard are there one minute and then disappear like ghosts in their arrival and departure in the dream. It's odd that I chose Chloe to form part of the plot. I believe she is a substitute for my daughter Rachael, as they are a similar age, and were close to each other when growing up as small children. It would be more appropriate for Rachael to be alongside me, if I was preparing to avoid a war.

When I think of the cost to fly to America, it does seem absurd that I would go there to purchase one roll of wallpaper. I also believe that a security guard could retrieve my money from an unknown character described as "the tramp". I assume the security guard will get the tramp by hunting him down, even though I didn't witness the robbery, or given him a description.

The act of considering my delusional beliefs led me to believe that there is not a shred of self-awareness to tell me that any of these convictions are true. This is despite the fact that I experienced them as authentic while dreaming. By considering the strange content of my dream, I can discard the "non-sensible features" of mine and the dream characters' thoughts, feelings and behaviours.

Feelings

In the dream

In the dream there are no specific references as to how I felt. I therefore must imagine my dreaming feelings. It's reasonable to assume that I should be worried about an impending war, and anxious about losing some money. After noticing that the money is gone, there are no descriptions of the alarm that one may experience in waking life following such a situation. A lack of panic continues when I casually stroll to a security hatch to report the loss, and I appear to accept the dream events as they unravel.

On waking

This absence of worry began to change when I viewed the dream from a waking perspective. On reflecting upon this dream, I experienced anxious feelings as I am trying to prevent something bad, i.e., a war happening, over which I have no control, and it involves losing money. I try to rectify this situation by enlisting the help of a security guard who agrees to retrieve my money.

The meaning of the dream

At the time of this dream I was contemplating leaving the NHS and giving up a safe job to promote my private practice. The loss of money in the dream reflects the loss of income from leaving a secure post in waking life. I wanted to leave the NHS because I didn't like the bureaucratic red tape that went with the job. All client work was dictated by a tick-box culture with the emphasis on short-term work for long standing mental health problems. This was sometimes unsatisfactory for clients, often putting me in a position of ending my work prematurely. I spoke about my concerns, but my voice was disregarded. This is the first insight from the dream.

The dream takes place in America during 1990 when we were not so politically correct, and individuals said what they thought, without fear of recrimination. In the dream I could appear discriminatory by today's standards, and raise a few eyebrows by associating the loss of my money with a tramp's involvement.

This power imbalance played an important role in identifying the next insight. A fear of tramps goes back to my childhood when sadly they were considered people to avoid, because they were labelled suspicious, smelly people who stole things. I realised later that the tramp represents the inequality I felt for some of the clients I worked with, who were being "robbed" of the appropriate support to get better. Whilst I have the utmost respect for the uniqueness of others, I also protest against the "powers-that-be" who try to silence other people's views. I couldn't continue working effectively with some of my NHS clients on short-term contracts. It bothered me that there was nowhere else for them to go, unless they paid for private therapy.

I concluded that my attempt to find the dream money was representative of the money I hoped would be forthcoming from developing my private practice in waking life. My dreaming mind concocted a dramatic scenario of theft, showing me that I would be worse off financially. Instead, in waking life I took a leap of faith by leaving the NHS, which ultimately led to a successful career.

At first glance my dream seems to be an example of illogical thoughts. I believe the reason Hobson's theory proved successful with this dream is because by removing the parts that didn't make sense, I was left with my dream-self's behaviour which seemed realistic. By introducing feelings at the end, this gives his approach the final touches to transform a confused dream into a coherent meaning. There is a lot of psychological meaning in this dream which I discovered directly and indirectly, without resorting to the decoding of Freudian dream symbols.

★ ★ ★

I differ from Hobson's view that dreams are random activity, because the evidence from all the dreams in this book so far points to strong links to waking experience. The process which appears random with this dream is the memory recall. If my recall occurred five minutes later, I may have reported a completely different dream.

Hobson's activation-synthesis theory provides a sound account of the brain mechanisms underlying REM sleep and dreaming. Basing a psychological interpretation on the physiology of the dream state does make his theory convincing. He has arguably been one of the dominant scientists in dream research for the past forty years, and I regard him as a worthy rival to Freud as one of the most important dream theorists ever.

Hobson is now embarking on another experiment. By stirring up the Holy Grail of scientific philosophy, he's investigating the mind/brain problem, and how brain chemistry influences the states of consciousness.[26] I look forward to reading what this remarkable man says about such an age-old conflict, and whether any new information affects the meaning of dreams.

## 7

Dreams Are Visual Metaphors that
Reflect our True Emotions

Readers may notice there are no UK contributions for any dream theories described in this book. I am about to change all that and fly the flag for Britain. Born in 1948 in Hornsea, in North Yorkshire, I spent much of my teenage years in London, when it was swinging with the arrival of British pop music, fashion and a new liberalism for young people. There were many jobs available at that time, and after being employed as a civil servant, a post-lady, a chamber maid, a factory hand, a barmaid, working in a garden centre and numerous office jobs, I drifted into a retail management scheme for a well-known chain store. This became my main career until I divorced my second husband.

Following my break-up, I sold my house in Surrey, took the proceeds from the sale and headed back to the north to start a new life. I started a cleaning business to fit around my daughters' school times. While chatting to one of my customers, a counsellor, I realised I wanted to do something similar. I subsequently embarked on a counselling training course at Leeds Metropolitan University (now Leeds Beckett University) during 1995.

After completing my training, I worked as a counsellor in the voluntary sector, in bereavement care, for the York NHS psychology department, as a freelance Employment Assistance Programme (EAP) counsellor and finally counselled young people in an education setting. I also started a private practice, and eventually trained to be a clinical supervisor. In my private capacity I counselled a male client who regularly brought his dreams for discussion, and his enthusiasm kickstarted me into taking my professional interest in this topic more seriously.

I enrolled on a Doctoral research programme to investigate whether it was helpful for clients to discuss dreams in therapy.[1] I found it was beneficial, but I also discovered the theories I studied weren't compatible with the way I worked. I therefore set out to develop another model, which was more suited to humanistic practitioners like myself. Humanistic practitioners recognise everyone's uniqueness, and assume that individuals have a capacity to grow emotionally, towards the goal of personal fulfilment.

Adam's Theoretical Approach

My personal and professional philosophies stem from the "Relational Model", (where all the parts are connected)[2] in which I originally trained as a counsellor. The Relational Model claims that relationships between people are the foundation for our individual and social lives, and it takes different social, political, and cultural influences into account when interacting with others.[3]

The approach I developed as a result of my Doctoral research was called "The Integrative Model", which was designed as a textbook model for other humanistic practitioners to use. However, while writing this textbook I realised I wanted to write for the general reader and scrapped it before it was published.

Adam's Integrative – Vision Model

The main source of inspiration that fuelled me to change my academic writing to a more creative style came after reading Ann Faraday's best seller *Dream Power*,[4] and her sequel, *Dream Game*,[5] both "how-to-interpret-your-own-dreams" guides. Faraday was way ahead of her time in making her PhD study on dream interpretation accessible to the general reader as well as the professional field, during the 1970s. I developed a further model for the general reader, calling it the "Integrative – Vision Model" which consists of the following beliefs:

- Dreams are personal to the dreamer.
- Dreams include thoughts and feelings which are represented metaphorically in dreams.
- Characters, objects and settings can be represented metaphorically in dreams.
- The dreamer's dream behaviour often mirror's waking life behaviour.

- Dreams express current preoccupations in waking life experience.
- Understanding dreams helps our relationships with ourselves and important others.

This model tries to overcome the weaknesses of the dream story, by expanding our dream thoughts and feelings and explaining our behaviour and speech patterns. By identifying these missing features, the model constructs a rational story for interpretation. The principle I shall follow is to explain the model of visualising a dream like a picture, and trying to relate that picture to a waking life situation.

Illustrated below are the aspects of a dream in which we interact. These consist of "tangible features", which we can visualise or hear in the dream, and are shown inside the bubble. "Abstract features" which we can't see are displayed outside the dream bubble, waiting to be identified.

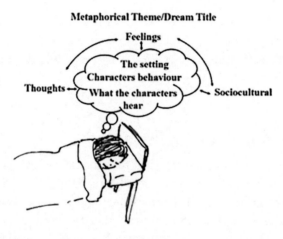

Figure 7.0 Adam's Integrative-Vision Model[6]

There are two types of tangible features which we experience that keep us in the reality of the dream experience. They are, visually, a description of the setting, and the behaviour of the dream characters. From an auditory perspective we can hear what the dream characters say. I have omitted the sensory perceptions of smell and taste, because they happen infrequently, and don't influence the meaning of a dream. With regards to touch, this is part of what we see, for example, 'He walked up to me, and put his arm around me'.

Abstract processes which we can't see, are our thoughts, our feelings and influences from our sociocultural environment consisting of our beliefs, values and attitudes. It's only through exploratory questions that these aspects come to life, and we can begin to understand them in relation to the dream story. When we make sense of this metaphorical imagery I believe we can identify our dream thoughts and feelings, which often represent relationships with ourselves and important others.

The Integrative–Vision model accommodates six interconnected levels of insight where all, or some of them may be linked. They are: (1) the dream setting; (2) the behaviour of the dream-self and characters or objects; (3) the dialogue spoken by the dream characters; (4) dream and waking thoughts, and links to waking experience; (5) dream and waking feelings, and links to waking experience; and (6) the sociocultural context (optional).

The dream setting

The dreaming mind creates a stage against which the dream plot can be played out. In sleep, we often have difficulty in creating a realistic set for the dream scenario given the many potential possibilities from a lifetime of experience. But sometimes the setting can reveal a clue to the meaning of a dream.

In waking life, while on holiday in Oslo during 2015, I narrowly avoided the Grim Reaper and his scythe-wielding invitation to join him in death. He came out of nowhere, and left me lying in a Norwegian hospital suffering from a cerebral stroke. With a heavy heart I tried to accept that fate had given me a raw deal. The next day Rachael flew out to see me, and that night I had a vivid dream which I called "The Blizzard".

> I'm in a familiar waking setting in Flaxton where Rachael lives. It's snowing very heavily, and I can't see where I am going. I manage to battle through the blizzard down the lane to the bus stop, where my grandsons get off the school bus. It's still snowing, and through the snow I see Sarah and say to her, 'This is for you'. I hand her an old cassette tape on which I've recorded some country and western songs she might like to hear (2015).

On waking, although I felt afraid, I still had cognitive functioning and thought about the dream setting. The snow was falling heavily outside my bedroom window in the hospital, and it was also snowing in my dream. This similarity helped me to discover the meaning of this dream. The reason I dreamt about Sarah was, because when Rachael arrived she sent a photo of me to Sarah who stayed in England to look after both sets of grandsons. We both share a love of music, and giving her a gift in the dream was my way of telling her to remember me how I was, before I had my stroke. Fortunately, I did recover due to the excellent care and support I received from Chrissy Gilham, the Consultants at the Rikshospitalet, and my two daughters during the early stages of my rehabilitation.

The behaviour of the dream-self and other characters or objects

The dream behaviour of ourselves can produce descriptions which can draw out our waking conflicts or achievements. As the dream is created by ourselves it is no surprise that we are usually in the leading role. However, sometimes we are accompanied by different dream figures, some of who we know, or others who feature as strangers. A demonstration of the significance of dream behaviour will be given when describing my own dream shortly.

The dialogue spoken by the dream characters

I believe we should pay attention to what the dream characters say to each other. In my dream of the blizzard, the remark 'This is for you', confirmed that the gift which I offered to Sarah had a hidden meaning of "remember me how I was". This proved important to me at that time.

Dream and waking thoughts, and links to waking experience

Ernest Hartmann, psychoanalyst and dream researcher, suggests that in waking life, the mind is a network of fishing nets.[7] He points out that while awake, if he wants to remember where he lived at a point in time, he searches his memory banks (the nets), until he finds a connection which relates to that particular house.[8]

In dreaming, his thinking is not as precise as when he's awake, as the connections are widespread and less concentrated. When dreaming about searching for a house, this may result in him looking for images of other houses and similar buildings such as hotels. Due to this indiscriminate way of searching for links, his thoughts lose their way, and latch onto anything remotely familiar.[9] Hartmann's final dream imagery could be borne out of a memory which is only partially related, or totally unconnected.

An example of this was reported in my baby boy dream in Chapter 6. I believe my dream state could not recognise one of my two younger grandsons (who took up my time), and chose at random a little boy of the same age. He may have been a toddler from my own childhood, or one of my grandsons' friends. Nevertheless, he served the purpose of being an unwanted burden, instead of my dream-self choosing another task that was getting in the way – my clinical work. Perhaps, by choosing an anonymous little boy, I felt less guilty about blaming my clients for preventing me from completing my thesis.

Dream and waking feelings, and links to waking experience

According to Hartmann, a dream metaphor is underpinned by a feeling influence. By placing emphasis on the feeling aspect of the metaphor, it becomes the dominant image, which he calls the "central image". It's often the clearest picture-metaphor to describe a dream,[10] and can be represented by a character, animal, object or the setting. Another one way to unearth the metaphor from a dream is to ask yourself what new light the central image sheds on a waking life situation.

My personalised dreams shown in previous chapters are now summarised, with their metaphorical central image showing corresponding feelings. The central image also acts as the dream title, which encapsulates the meaning of the dream, in the same way artists choose titles to showcase their paintings.

Table 7.0 Metaphorical Central Images and Underlying Feelings

Chapter	Central Image	Underlying Feelings
1	Nora	Sadness associated with remembering Nora.
1	The Post-Box	Anger for two of my employers.
2	Awards Ceremony	Anxiety regarding my BSc awards ceremony.
3	The Black Dog	Sadness and fear about Tina being put to sleep.
3	Snow-Capped Mountains	Sadness and fear concerning a relationship.
4	Nellie the Elephant	Fear about wanting to retire.
5	The Grim Reaper	Fear concerning the Grim Reaper's role.
5	The Wild Boar	Anger towards someone in waking life.
5	The Disappearing Policeman	Sad feelings in relation to someone from my past.
5	A Stranger	Fearful of being attacked.

Chapter	Central Image	Underlying Feelings
5	President Trump	Disgust at Trump trying it on with me.
5	A Visit in London	Anxiety about being lost in London.
5	An African Holiday	Sadness associated with a previous holiday.
5	The Missing Station	Feeling sad in waking life.
5	The Secret Service	Happiness about my trip to Bletchley Park Museum.
5	On the Beach	Anxiety about leaving Daisy.
5	Old Friends	Happiness when remembering two friends.
5	The Story	Sad that I can't write this book.
6	The Headmistress	Happiness remembering my school days.
6	A Baby Boy	Fear of not getting my thesis completed.
6	Morrisons	Anxiety about Sarah not getting fed.
6	The Money	Fear regarding a potential loss of income.
7	The Blizzard	Sadness that Sarah will not know me.

Although I used different theories to interpret some of these dreams, I have backtracked to determine what feelings accompany the main image of the dreams. These feelings become my "waking emotions" that the dreams are trying to communicate to me. I could end my dream model at this point. However, because my philosophy acknowledges sociocultural differences, I think it's important to have another level which reflects these characteristics.

A sociocultural context (optional)

Montague Ullman, a psychiatrist and psychoanalyst who dedicated much of his work to extending dream-work for the public, suggests dreams contain "personal referents" (thoughts, feelings, and behaviour) which disclose our current preoccupations. At the same time, they contain another unconscious layer which he calls "social referents",[11] which communicate the unsolved problems of the society we live in. We're usually unaware of our social referents as we don't connect our dream images to society's problems, because they are beyond our immediate concern[12] I believe our social referents lie deeper than our dream thoughts and emotions, and consists of our beliefs, values, and attitudes which can also influence our dreams. Ullman claims that identifying our social referents provides insight into the way that problems can only be resolved through a societal level.[13]

The Senoi Tribe

I will now take a detour to discuss the Senoi, one of the most famous examples of a tribe who apply their beliefs to determine the meaning of their dreams. The Senoi people are made up of two groups called the Temiar and the Semia, who are ethnically linked and live in the mountainous jungles of Malaysia. This dream philosophy was made famous by Kilton Stewart. He claims in his paper, *Dream Theory in Malaya*,[14] that the Senoi's techniques of controlling the outcome of their dreams resulted in no mental illness or violence, and an increased sexual pleasure in waking life. These beliefs made them amongst the happiest and healthiest people in the world.

Stewart amplified the Senoi practices to such an extent that his claims were practiced by health professionals of the dream-work movement at the Esalen Institute during 1965. Subsequently Senoi dream philosophy became increasingly popular amongst the general public, largely due to two authors at that time. It featured in Faraday's two books previously described, where she claims that she practised the Senoi techniques. Stewart's claim was also backed up by psychologist Patricia Garfield who wrote *Creative Dreaming*,[15] a publication about primitive cultures' meaning of dreams. She outlined the Senoi dream theory after she had spoken to some of the tribe at a hospital in Gombak, Malaysia.

Summarised below are the three principles which underpin the Senoi practices from the Stewart–Garfield camp. The first principle is that the tribe always "confront and conquer danger in dreams". If someone the dreamer knows in waking life appears violent in the dream, the dreamer needs to defeat them and even kill them to win. Garfield describes in one dream how she and her youngest daughter are being chased by a gang of youths who intend to rape them. She remembers to confront and conquer them, by turning around and spraying something into their eyes. This enables her and her daughter to escape. She describes how using this technique in her dreams made her feel less helpless in waking life when facing tricky situations.[16]

The second principle is that with sexual dreams the tribe "move towards a pleasurable experience and should intensify such pleasure" until they have an orgasm, irrespective of who is involved in the activity. Garfield reports that before using Senoi practices, she sometimes did have orgasms in dreams when she was deprived of sexual contact, or during times when she was particularly sexually active. By allowing her sexual dream experience to continue, she experienced more orgasms in waking life,[17] although tantalisingly she doesn't divulge her techniques of influencing a dream in this way.

As I haven't mastered this technique of what appears to be lucid dreaming, I can't suggest a way to achieve orgasms while dreaming. If I have dreamt of having sex with friends or colleagues, I see that as a harmless fantasy, and wouldn't want to replicate that experience in waking life.

The last principle is that the Senoi should make sure "their dreams have an agreeable outcome, and they extract a creative product from them", such as a song, painting or poem. In a dream, the way to achieve this is by obtaining a gift from anyone who appears hostile. Garfield wishes that she had asked her attackers previously described for a gift, to finish her dream in a positive way.[18]

Faraday initially echoes the views of Stewart and Garfield and acknowledges that she practiced this theory, by changing terrifying dreams when she was falling into pleasurable experiences. In *The Dream Game* she justified the Senoi's theory by claiming that while dreaming, if an aggressive topdog image appears, she tries to subdue it before it can become her friend. If the hostile image is an underdog, she confronts it until it becomes less antagonistic.[19] By training herself to use these techniques in her dreams, she reduced the number of nightmares that she had.

Faraday later had a change of heart about what she had written. After spending time visiting the Senoi during 1982–83 with her husband, they reported that not one single Temiar recalled any form of dream control, and denied that manipulating dreams was ever part of their cultural practices.[20] I admire Faraday for stating that everything she had previously written on the basis of Stewart's explanation was inaccurate.

This theory continued to provoke a lot of controversy, and by the late 1980s Bill Domhoff challenged the Stewart-Garfield claims both on his website[21] and in his book, *The Mystique of Dreams: A Search for Utopia through Senoi Dream Theory*.[22] He suggests this tribe do try to avoid conflict in their waking life, but it's untrue that they are never violent, or that their physical and mental health is considered remarkable.[23] He reports the Temiar tribe would guide slave traders to Semia and other Temiar settlements, knowing the traders would murder many of the adults. He also suggests that mental illness does exist. At a hospital in Gombak, nine Senoi were treated during the early seventies for psychotic symptoms.[24]

Domhoff believes that Stewart's claim of the Senoi expressing sexual love in a dream appears to be a contradiction. He cites Stewart as introducing the notion that pleasurable dreams should reach a natural conclusion,[25] whereas in Stewart's earlier dissertation,[26] his discussions on sexual dreams doesn't mention dreams culminating in orgasms. Domhoff states it is Stewart who reports that individuals may be able to control their dreams to enhance pleasure and psychological health in waking life, and suggests Stewart's and Garfield's views are a fairy-tale. However, Domhoff hasn't observed the Senoi tribe directly, and bases his argument on other anthropologists' claims and by talking to relatives and friends of Stewart.

The Senoi dream techniques were practised and demonstrated very clearly by Garfield and Faraday, who both said they work. Maybe the Americans were open to happy endings during the mid-sixties, a time of freedom, and one way of achieving this was through manipulating their dreams. I don't know who to believe. Either way, by writing about the Senoi, I now hold the opinion that there are other cultures who don't share a similar view of dreaming which I and the other theorists preach. I am appreciative of this fact, which is mirrored by Edgar and Tedlock in Chapter 1, and for this reason I have added a sociocultural perspective to my model.

The grass roots of a dream

I went to sleep during late November 2016 thinking about how I could demonstrate a social referent from one of my dreams. The next morning, I awoke feeling anxious, after having the following dream which I called "A Simple Room".

> I'm in an old warehouse with Sarah and we are clearing out a room for me to have as a bedroom. It's full of old furniture and lawnmowers. I say, 'I want this room to be simple so that no one will come and rob me'. Then I show her a belt that I've bought her for Christmas. It has a big buckle and it is embossed with a banjo and fiddle, and is similar to the belts that cowboys and cowgirls wear. I think that she can wear it at the 2017 Country to Country Festival at the O2 in London. I say, 'It's a bargain as I got it reduced to £40.00' (2016).

The previous day I was round at Sarah's house when she asked me if I wanted to stay with her after my short stay in hospital. This would happen two weeks later. I believe this dream reflects an anxiety about leaving my bungalow unattended. By having an uncluttered room similar to my bungalow I must have thought while dreaming this would remove some of the temptation for thieves to rob me.

The social referent for this dream is identified by acknowledging that there exists an anxiety towards an increase in theft. To do something constructive about this message in waking life I could have got involved in the local neighbourhood watch scheme to combat crime. I didn't, because it didn't occur to me to do so.

Exploring the grass roots of my dream provided me with an increased insight about myself. As a retired counsellor I think I'm an aware being, and was surprised that identifying a social referent had revealed another realm of reality to add to my existing knowledge – a deeper truth.

Personalised Dream Interpretation: The Post-Box

I will now demonstrate the techniques using the Integrative–Vision model

> I'm in a department store where I used to work as an assistant store manager in my younger days. I want some lunch from the restaurant, but there is nothing left. I go into the kitchen and see a member of staff, Ann. She apologises because she is short-staffed. This makes me angry and I ask her to cook me some food. Then I take some documents which I want to post that are confidential. I don't want anyone to see them, so I shove them in a rucksack and leave the building. Next, I'm walking down a country lane and spot a red post-box, but I don't post the documents. I want a bus to come along as it's too far to walk. Then I see a country pub and go inside to get some food. It looks like a Chinese buffet, and the chef has ginger hair and a moustache. I ask him how much the buffet is, and he replies, '£23.99'. I think this is too expensive and say, 'Its daylight robbery', and we have a massive argument (2008).

This dream was also featured in Chapter 1 were I pointed out that there are several things missing from the dream to enable me to understand its meaning. They are: the fact that the dream scenes are not continuous, there is no explanation for the reason I chose not to post the confidential documents, and there is no conclusion to the dream, i.e., I don't say what happened next. I will attempt to answer these questions.

Draw the dream

The drawing of the dream is optional for readers, and I suggest you do this if there is more than one scene.

Figure 7.1 Post-Box Dream[27]

The dream will be explored from questions relating to the six different insight levels previously described. I will use Interpretive Phenomenological Analysis (IPA)[28] to interpret the insights from each level. IPA is a psychological research approach which aims to offer insights into how a person makes sense of a specific topic that relates to experiences of personal significance. Think of this task as sorting out the "wood" from the "trees", where we separate important themes from those which are less relevant. The main themes are shown below in italics and will be transferred to the final analysis later on.

How does the dream setting connect to waking life experience?

The dream setting was a work-based environment. *The kitchen is similar to the kitchen in the department store where I worked twenty-five years before I had this dream.* I didn't recognise the country road or the outside of the pub, although the inside is similar to a Chinese buffet I frequent in waking life.

How does the behaviour of the characters or objects connect to a waking situation?

Ann is apologetic because she can't feed me. After I have put the confidential documents in a ruck sack I dither around on seeing a post-box and decide not to post them. I eventually go into a pub and have a massive argument with the chef who I will call Peter.

The behaviour of these two characters reminded me of a conversation I had on the telephone with two counsellors, during the course of the previous evening. I was freelancing as an employee assistance programme (EAP) provider at the time of this dream counselling employees who had been referred for therapy by their company. I went to bed the night before after arguing on the phone with a female counsellor and her male boss. I had requested more time to finish a contract satisfactorily with a vulnerable client, and behind my back they contacted my client to check that my request was justified. Needless to say, my client was upset as their actions breached the confidentiality code I implemented.

What do the dream characters say to each other?

There is an exchange between my dream-self and Peter. *He says, 'It's £23.99 for a buffet lunch'. I reply, 'It's daylight robbery'.*

What are the dreamer's dream and waking thoughts, and links to waking experience?

Thoughts in the dream

I thought Ann was inefficient for running out of food. I considered that Peter was untrustworthy by trying to charge me a "rip-off" price for a buffet lunch. I appear indecisive about posting the documents, by saying *'I want to post them', and then on approaching the post-box, 'I don't post them'.*

How are these thoughts connected to waking life?

Thinking about the role of the two characters didn't mean anything to me at this stage of interpreting the dream. In waking life I recognised that my indecision regarding either to post the documents or not, was the waking life equivalent of whether to give up a lucrative contract or just toe-the-line and do nothing.

What are the dreamer's dream and waking feelings, and links to waking experience?

Feelings in the dream

My dream-self shows anger towards Ann and Peter for not providing me with any food, and the exorbitant price Peter wants to charge me for a buffet lunch.

How are these feelings connected to waking life?

When I got in touch with my waking feelings everything fell into place. The personality characteristics of the dream characters were the same as the two counsellors I had argued with during the previous evening. I regarded the female counsellor who was apologetic about not extending my contract was represented by Ann, as incompetent (Ann was inefficient in waking life). Her boss, depicted as Peter, was untrustworthy as he was the one who had the last say and ultimately refused my request. *I felt angry, because of the casual treatment I received from two counsellors on such an important ethical issue.*

What is the social referent of the dream?

I was in the same boat as many of my colleagues who had to terminate short-term contracts with clients who needed long-term support. If I knew about the social referent impacting on my dream, I could have tried to find my client a suitable replacement counsellor for free.

An integration of the categories

Having decided the main themes by italicising them, place them in one of two categories: dream or waking life experience in chronological order of the insight levels.

Dream experience

- The kitchen is similar to the kitchen in the department store where I worked twenty-five years before I had this dream.
- He says, 'It's £23.99 for a buffet lunch'. I reply, 'It's daylight robbery'.
- 'I want to post them', and then on approaching the post-box, 'I don't post them'.
- My dream-self shows anger towards Ann and Peter.

Waking life experience

- The behaviour of these two characters reminded me of a conversation I had on the telephone with two counsellors, during the course of the previous evening.
- I felt angry, because of the casual treatment I received from two counsellors on such an important ethical issue.
- I was in the same boat as many of my colleagues who had to terminate short-term contracts with clients who needed long-term support.

My dream is expanded by identifying thoughts and feelings that were either missing or unclear in the dream, and by analysing the dream characters' behaviour and speech patterns. These processes were identified and integrated by separating dream reality from a reflective waking perspective. This ensures a more accurate interpretation of the post-box dream which I described as "thin" in Chapter 1, and now appears to be a whole lot "fatter".

The meaning of the dream

An integration of dreaming and waking life experience enabled me to choose the main parts of the dream which matter, irrespective of the fact that the scenes weren't connected. I asked myself 'What does integrating the themes tell me about my experience of these characters or object, and the situation?' The dream carries two important meanings.

Firstly, the post-box is an expression for my dilemma about whether to lodge a complaint or not to the EAP agency. I realised that my conscience, which remained absent in the dream, was important to acknowledge in waking life. I also felt cheated in waking life by the company who didn't give me a chance to finish my work ethically.

Secondly, I felt short-changed by not being "fed" on two separate occasions – in the dream by Ann and Peter. I didn't trust them, and by feeling hungry at the end of the dream, I was still "not feeling satisfied" with the way the situation had been concluded.

What action, if any, is required as a result of the dream?

Not all dreams lend themselves to some form of action. Asking what you want to change in the dream, can quickly determine if there is a need for a difference to take place in waking life experience. I did complain to the counselling agency about the breach in ethics, completed the short contract with this client, and subsequently resigned from the EAP provider.

★ ★ ★

The Integrative–Vision model is in the early stages of development, and hasn't been empirically tested. I maintain its strengths are that it can be used by different cultures, and it's useful for analysing dreams with many unstructured scenes. It has been used by family, friends, other counsellors, and supervisors, where I have received positive feedback.

There may be some critics who say my methods are biased, because I applied my own dreams to demonstrate the techniques in this book. I helped many former clients to interpret their dreams, but I didn't want to use their dreams as I respected their trust in me to maintain confidentiality. The only way I could be truly authentic about the techniques I use is to describe my own dreams. This proved a daunting proposition in which I exposed a lot of personal information. In the end I put my fear to one side, and listened to Lizzi Linklater, my creative writing tutor, and her inspiring words to 'Get on with it'.

8

Summing-Up of the Theories

The secrets of dreams and their meanings have challenged humankind throughout history and continue to do so. That's because our dreams often present us with a puzzling display of images which at first glance can't be understood. If we don't pay attention to these images and try to understand what they are telling us, then we are neglecting what may be our most powerful resource for personal growth.

Dreams are presented in a situation staged within a setting, often with ourselves as observers and sometimes as a participant along with a variety of other characters and objects. Our dream-selves along with the characters, carry out various activities and interactions, but dreams lack the clarity of the waking perceptions, thoughts and emotions we use to determine our ongoing behaviour.

Dreams can't be seen by others and are reported by ourselves on waking. This can result in a haphazard recounting, as once we are awake we have already interfered with the evidence of the dream, by recalling it from hazy memory. This runs the risk that we may embellish our dreams, or leave things out. For us to understand our dreams, we need to transform our dream features into an organised process. To achieve this, we are required to mentally create a coherent story, to facilitate understanding about this experience, and finally reach new insights.

However, we are faced with two opposing realities from a single dream event. While dreaming, we experience the event as real, but on waking we convert these experiences to a complete fabrication. Trying to reconcile these two conflicting positions requires a systematic method, as our rational logic will not suffice. The search to unravel these images has caused a great deal of speculation, with numerous theories having their day, and then disappearing for good.

A summing up of the theories

There are some theories that have stood the test of time, such as the theories provided by Freud,[1] Jung,[2] Perls,[3] and Hall and Nordby.[4] These theories and my own model[5] propose that dreams carry important psychological information. That's because when we interpret our dreams by using these techniques they invariably produce meaningful associations to past, current or future waking preoccupations. On the other hand, Hobson claims that dreams should be examined from a physiological perspective, which may enable us to detect underlying personality conflicts.[6]

I now invite you to consider all the theories by reading the summaries, and using the dream journals shown at the back of this book for the ones that you prefer, to interpret your dreams. The dream journals are in the same format as the stages that are shown in each chapter for the individual theorists.

Freud: Free Association

Freud claims that dreams are disguised wish fulfilments that reside in our unconscious minds. The disguised true dream, known as the latent content, is changed to a memory called the manifest content, by the time we wake up. The dream is camouflaged mainly by two different processes of the dream-work – condensation and displacement. There is no evidence to suggest that dreams do go through this transformation.

Freud's task as an analyst was to help his patients to reveal their latent thoughts in order to disclose their unfulfilled wishes. To achieve this, he applied his technique of free association to their manifest content, which dissected every individual sentence of the dream. After a lengthy recycling job of free association, he interpreted the new latent images as consisting of a probable sexual nature. His interpretations originate from working with a group of neurotic female patients, or his own dreams, and can be seen as biased. Once Freud's patients had succumbed to his talking cure, they would be rid of their undesirable thoughts, and any symptoms regarding an illness would disappear.

Freud focused on generating much information unrelated to the original dream, and he made no reference to emotion, a fundamental experience of dreaming and waking existence. Most people narrate their dream content with many visual images, but Freud placed little emphasis on visual imagery.

I have followed Freud's techniques for personalised dream interpretation. It's the introduction of the unconscious into dreams that Freud is remembered for. Neuroscience has demonstrated that there is far more going on in the mind than researchers were previously aware of. They now know that an aspect of experience exists which isn't in our conscious awareness.[7] By considering dreams as originating from the unconscious, we can access important information which was previously unavailable. This can identify hidden aspects of our personalities that we may wish to change in waking life.

So, was Freud an ambitious man who used his approach to satisfy his fantasies about his female patients, and set out to dominate the psychology field with his wish fulfilment theory? Or was he an articulate, literary genius who, for the first time, revealed the unconscious mind as a way of getting to the true source of a dream? If so, this makes his ideas a landmark in understanding the potential of dreams as a tool for personal thoughts and insight, and makes him one of the greatest thinkers of the twentieth century.

Jung: Amplification

Jung's theory claims dreams are messages from our higher, wiser self, and they compensate for something missing in our lives. He believes the manifest content contains the whole meaning, and its purpose is to reveal deep insights about our personalities that are spiritually important to us. To understand the meaning of a dream, we must explore our dream imagery through amplification in conjunction with one, two, and/or three levels of the mind.

In the first level, we associate selected dream objects with personal meanings that are connected to a dream image. If a meaning is not forthcoming, we move into the second level which looks for a cultural connection to the same dream image. If this level doesn't yield any new insight, we move into the final stage. In the third and much deeper level, we use archetypal images from myths and folklore which are part of the collective unconscious to give symbolic meaning to our dream image. We go through the different levels of amplification till we reach a meaning which "clicks" as being right, and then use this new-found knowledge to move towards individuation, a state of feeling whole to achieve our maximum potential.

Jung: Active Imagination

Jung's other technique of obtaining meaning from a dream was the rewriting of a dream report using active imagination. The dream is presented as a book with four main parts: the setting and context, the development of the plot, conflict on behalf of the dreamer, and the outcome. Jung suggests the outcome is the most crucial of all the scenes because it shows us how to deal with a problem that happened in the first part of the dream.

This process allows our dream elements to come into our awareness naturally and lets us treat them as though they are real. Our dream-self interacts with these elements with the intention of getting to know them by imagining what they have to say. We listen to their responses and imagine our reply. Once we have an awareness of the message from the dream, an interpretation is reached by considering the thoughts and feelings from each level, and relating them to waking life experience. This usually involves us changing the way we relate to someone or something.

Jung's discovery of the collective unconscious has expanded our understanding of the mysterious world of the unconscious. However, there is no proof that the mind is split in the way he suggests, and that the collective unconscious actually exists. One doubt I have about Jung's first approach, is whether it would work as well with a lengthy, complicated dream. With dreams that consist of several scenes, I suggest active imagination would be more suitable, as it quickly enables us to focus on the main themes.

Jung was branded by some as having unscientific thinking, playing dangerously close to the occult, concentrating solely on the self, and not paying enough attention to waking relationships. Others see his legacy as using dreams to express our emotions. If this is the case then it makes Jung one of the most distinguished figures in psychology, for identifying this important resource from exploring our dreams.

Perls: Roleplay

Perls suggests every object and character in a dream represents fragmented aspects of our personalities. Fragmentation is caused by the anxiety we experience when we are being phony, which is conveyed by the things we say, chicken-shit, bull-shit, or elephant-shit. We do this to deny the truth about our feelings. Perls claims that we need to stop acting as phonies, and take responsibility for any underlying feelings which may lead to inner conflict.

To understand a dream meaning it is necessary to isolate at least two of the characters or objects from a dream, and get them to speak to each other as our topdog and underdog personalities. The dialogue continues with the empty-chair technique until a conflict emerges. Then a battle commences between topdog and underdog until we reach a compromise, when a new insight is reached. This new insight creates a truce with the dogs, which results in the two personalities who were previously at war now existing side by side. Our disowned personalities then become integrated, and any anxiety is removed.

Perls' approach is easily transferable for those who wish to explore their dreams alone, as the methods are simplistic. Dialogues with dream characters using the empty-chair technique can sometimes lead to insights, which would not be available through simply describing our dreams.

This approach would not work as well with long dreams containing many dream characters or objects. Perls suggests that, with these type of dreams, a small aspect is chosen to work with instead. His view is extremely ambitious, because the same characters with whom we interact in waking life are denied any objective reality in the dream story. This means when characters are perceived as fragmented parts of personalities, the way they behave in the dream may not reflect the actual qualities of the real people in waking life. As Perls wanted to conduct his interactions with his patients in the here-and-now experience, it meant the past was forbidden territory, and this limits the scope of his techniques.

Was Perls a therapist who humiliated his patients then bragged about it, and played to an audience to bolster his popularity? Or was he a shrewd, charismatic actor who developed a technique which quickly raised his patients' awareness? By creating an argument between his patient's topdog and underdog personalities, any conflict will be revealed by following the same speech pattern as if his patients were having a disagreement in waking life. Ultimately, this led to his patients recognising and changing unwanted aspects of their personalities, by taking responsibility for their phony speech and behaviour.

Hall and Nordby: Content Analysis

The method of content analysis entails removing some of the content that make up a series of dreams, and classifying them into categories of: the characters, social interactions between ourselves and other characters, objects that appear in the dream, the settings, the failures and successes that we have, the misfortunes and fortunes that happen to us, and the explicit emotions felt by us when dreaming. These categories are then compared to other dreams from a similar period to show the similarities. These results are correlated to a list of questions to determine what they may mean to us.

Neutral interactions are not included in the analysis and could affect the overall dream's meaning, and is an area for future research. However, using content analysis to interpret a series of dreams does highlight some of our current preoccupations, and aspects of our personalities which can lead to greater self-understanding. This gives us an opportunity to change things in our waking life if we wish to do so.

Hobson: A Formal Analysis

Hobson's activation-synthesis theory is a neurobiological model which claims dreams aren't psychologically motivated at all. The motivating force is nothing more than the physiological responses and brain processes that randomly occur usually during REM sleep. Hobson rejects the idea that dream research is based on their content. Instead, he states that dream studies should occupy the formal aspects of our dreaming mental states, so we can remove the individual distractions that exist in mental content.

Hobson concludes that five formal classifications make up a dream's structure which are amnesia, which occurs after a dream takes place, hallucinatory visual imagery which is also generally vivid, illogical thinking, delusional acceptance of the dream being authentic while dreaming, and strong emotions which may or may not be associated with our dreams.

His theory doesn't attempt to anticipate or explain the specific meaningful content of our dreams. However, the activation-synthesis model says that our dreams may mirror aspects of our personalities or current concerns, because dream imagery is synthesised from information that is housed in our memories.

There is no general consensus as to what the physiological purpose of dreams are. A major strength of Hobson's model is that it can be tested and potentially be discredited by research evidence. Another advantage is that he draws specific attention to a dreamer's emotion which is such an important part of human experience. I have demonstrated this with an interpretation of a dream of my own.

Is Hobson's theory a way of prolonging the long-standing battle he has with Freudian theory, or is he correct when he claims that by applying his formal classifications to a dream, we can identify valuable conflictual personality themes, without resorting to Freudian symbolism?

Adam: The Integrative–Vision Model

I believe dreams are visual metaphors which reflect our true thoughts and feelings. By examining our metaphorical imagery and understanding its language we can determine important relationships with ourselves and important others. The Integrative–Vision Model consists of six interconnected levels of insight, and can be viewed from: the dream setting, the behaviour of ourselves and the dream characters or objects, the dialogue spoken by ourselves and the dream characters, our dream, and waking thoughts, our dream, and waking feelings, and our sociocultural context.

All this information is coded into smaller pieces of dream meaning by using IPA[8] which divides the dream reality from our waking reflections. The dream is interpreted by us, after considering the essence of our thoughts, feelings and behaviour from these two categories. Once an interpretation feels right, we can then investigate whether there are any links to a waking life situation, which may require change.

I do believe my approach distinguishes it from the other theories by embracing all aspects of waking human experience, particularly behaviour and speech patterns, into the dream questions. The sociocultural context, which is optional, means this model can be used by different cultures. I do envisage that if this model is used widely, then I will receive feedback on ways to improve it.

## 9

A Reader's Do-It-Yourself Model

You may or may not agree with everything I have put forward as facts in this book. For those of you who aren't convinced by the theories in this book there is an opportunity for you to develop your own model by reading this chapter. I will demonstrate how I developed my theory through a criterion of different stages.

Stage 1: What is the Purpose of Dreaming?

I believe some dreams are unfulfilled wishes as suggested by Freud. I don't agree they are fragments of our personalities as claimed by Perls, or with Hobson's theory that they are random brain activities. There is no scientific proof to suggest that these two claims are true, nor have my dreams within the theorists' individual chapters fallen into either of these two categories. Nevertheless, by adapting all their approaches I reached a satisfactory conclusion to my dreams.

I'm convinced that some dreams carry a message from our unconscious, and can therefore be classed as coming from our higher, wiser selves as claimed by Jung. This is evident with my snow-capped mountains dream. I also believe that Hall and Nordby's techniques of interpreting a series of dreams generates increased self-knowledge. This is obvious with the summary of my results, which left me with additional insights about my dreams.

It's now known that important relationships we experience in our waking life influence our behaviour towards those people and others.[1] Given that our dream behaviour often mirrors what's going on in our waking world, then it's reasonable to assume that relationships also affect our dream behaviour. Hence my theory that dreams are visual metaphors which reflect our relationships with ourselves and significant others. This is the case with many of the events shown in my dreams.

For those of you who wish to expand your horizons in this area, I propose you access the website for the International Association for the Study of Dreams.[2] Here, you will find an abundance of other theories on the nature and meaning of dreams, through its academic journal *Dreaming,* and the magazine *Dream time.*

Stage 2: Areas to Focus On

In this stage your attention should be on the past, present or future areas of your waking life, or all three. This choice will determine the questions you will ask later. Freud chose his patient's past, while Jung, Perls, Hall and Nordbury, and Hobson seem to focus on the dreamer's present situation. I chose all three as I wanted greater flexibility – to look at the past, and see if the dream was impacting on the present, and if it could affect my future in my waking world.

Stage 3: Goals of the Dream-Work

For this third stage you need to decide whether you want to work on your dream experiences related to thoughts, emotions, and/or behaviour. Some of you will be better suited to concentrating on thoughts, whereas others may prefer to stick with emotions, and/or behaviour. I opted for all three as I believe that unconscious thoughts and emotions influence a dream's narrative, and cause us to behave in a particular way during the dream. I suggest all these processes are entwined in our sociocultural world.

Stage 4: Questions for Interpreting Dreams

The final stage is the most difficult because it covers the practical aspects of what questions you ask of yourself. I hope I have now made it clear that it is the enquiries we apply to a dream which produce the answers to the dream meaning. I have summarised the questions relating to my model which exist of open questions consisting of how, who and what. These types of questions prove most beneficial for asking a respondent to think and reflect, and to give their opinions and feelings on the topic being discussed. The questions also act as a link to waking experience to promote further self-understanding, and to provide any changes in waking life.

Table 9.0 Integrative–Vision Model and Influences

Applications	Which theory
Draw the dream.	Jung.
Reflections from the drawing.	Jung.
How does the dream setting connect to waking life experience?	Hall and Nordby, Delaney.
How does the behaviour of the characters connect to a waking situation?	Hall and Nordby, Perls, Hobson.
What do the dream characters say to each other?	Hall and Nordby.
What are the thoughts in the dream?	Freud, Jung, Perls, Hobson, Delaney, Hartmann.
How are these thoughts connected to waking life?	Freud, Jung, Perls, Hobson, Delaney, Hartmann.
What are the feelings in the dream?	Jung, Perls, Hall and Nordby, Hobson, Delaney, Hartmann.
How are these feelings connected to waking life?	Jung, Perls, Hobson, Delaney.
What is the social referent that is shared with others?	Ullman.
What action is required in waking life?	Perls, Hall and Nordby.

For those readers who would like to see a range of other questions in addition to the ones I have previously outlined throughout the chapters, I recommend the following publications: *Dream Power*,[3] *Dream Game*,[4] *The Individual and his Dreams*,[5] *Breakthrough Dreaming*,[6] and *Let Your Body Interpret Your Dreams*.[7] Developing your own theory will seem like taking on an experiment, but that is the nature of the "dream beast". For this reason, it may take some time for you to develop a model, but try to be patient.

I have provided you with a snapshot of one physiological, and five psychological theories which I have modified for personal use. I don't claim to have solved the never-ending enigma that is attached to explaining the meaning of dreams. However, by researching earlier theories, I've discovered that my dreams are easier to interpret. Most of my dreams featured in this publication carry some form of conflict, which I wouldn't have recognised if I hadn't interpreted them in the way I suggest. I then transferred any new insights resulting from interpreting my dreams into my waking life, and made appropriate changes for the good.

Writing *The Dream Interpreters* has proved challenging, but there's something unfinished for me about the business of dreaming. However, it won't be me who is searching for answers to what dreams mean in the future, as I'm moving onto my next project. Finally, if I have succeeded in transferring my research into a resource that is helpful for you to know more about your dreams, then the enlightening journey of writing this book will be a reward in itself.

Appendix A

Dream Interpretation: Free Association

1. **Write the dream report**

2. **Split the manifest content into small phrases**

3. **Free associate thoughts to the manifest phrases**

    What springs to mind when you think of this person, this image or this situation?

4. **Change the manifest phrases to the latent content**

    What else do these new phrases remind you of?

5. **Free associate to the latent content**

    What does each latent phrase tell you about yourself?

6. **The meaning of the dream**

    The meaning of the dream is revealed by summarising the latent themes.

Appendix B

Dream Interpretation: Amplification

1. **Write the dream report**

2. **Draw the dream**

    Choose the scene where your energy wants to go. Make a note of any reflections.

3. **Explore your images**

4. **Personal association**

    Choose one image and make a personal association to it. Record thoughts and feelings.

5. **Cultural association**

    How would an outsider describe this image? Record thoughts and feelings.

6. **Archetypal association**

    What is the symbolic meaning of the image? Record thoughts and feelings.

7. **The meaning of the dream**

    List the thoughts and feelings that occurred at each stage of the amplification process. An accumulation of these processes will reveal the dream message.

Appendix C

Dream Interpretation: Active Imagination

1. **Write the dream report**

2. **Draw a mandala (optional)**

3. **The introduction**

   Introduce the setting, the main characters, what they are doing and the situation.

4. **The development of the plot**

   Describe the emergence of the plot.

5. **The conflict**

   Outline the conflict, or something significant that happens in the dream.

6. **The outcome**

   Report the outcome of the dream and link it to the introduction part.

7. **The meaning of the dream**

   Link any thoughts and feelings to waking experience with a statement of, 'I realise the dream reflects/reminds me of/is similar to (a waking situation)'.

Appendix D

Dream Interpretation: Roleplay

1. **Write the dream report**

2. **Rewrite the dream in the first person, present tense**

    Put in italics anything that is added or different.

3. **Choose two of the images and have an imaginary dialogue**

    Describe the dialogue, paying attention to your body language and tone of voice.

4. **Identify the holes**

    Observe your current thoughts and emotions, as you reflect on the dialogue.

5. **Recognising the impasse**

    What's making you stuck?

6. **Freeing the impasse**

    An impasse is freed when your dogs reach a compromise.

7. **New insights**

    New insights are identified when you recognise the reasons for the underlying conflict.

8. **The meaning of the dream**

    Make an interpretation based on what you have learnt in the insight stage.

9. **What action, if any, is needed in waking life?**

Appendix E

Dream Interpretation: Content Analysis

1. **Categorise the dream reports**

2. **Answer the following questions that are appropriate to your results**

a) *Characters*

How many strangers, including unknown animals, are in the dreams?

Do the strangers who appear in your dreams remind you of people you know?

Do any of the strangers represent conflicting parts of your personality?

Do any of the animals represent parts of your personality?

How many characters, including known animals, are in the dreams?

Do the characters you dream about repeatedly represent your feelings for them?

What roles do famous people and mythical characters play in your dreams?

b) *Social interactions*

Do you appear as the victim or aggressor in aggressive interactions?

Do you initiate or receive most of the aggressive or friendly interactions?

Do the sexual partners in your dreams coincide with your sexual partners in waking life?

Do you initiate or receive most of the sexual encounters?

c) **Settings**

Are there more outdoor or indoor settings?

Are the settings familiar or unfamiliar?

What do they remind you of?

d) **Objects**

What objects are frequently repeated in the dream series?

What do these objects tell you about yourself?

Are there any objects you would like to remove or change, and why?

e) **Failure and success**

Do you have more successes than failures?

What did you do in your dream to achieve the successes?

What did you do in your dream to fail to achieve a goal?

What do these failures or successes remind you of in waking life?

f) **Misfortune and good fortune**

Do you have more misfortunes or good fortunes?

What happened in the dream to cause a misfortune?

What happened in the dream to cause a good fortune?

What do these misfortunes or good fortunes remind you of in waking life?

g) **Emotion**

What is it about the dream events or characters that make you feel angry, confused, disgusted, fearful (including being anxious), happy, sad or surprised.

What is the most dominant emotion and what does it tell you about yourself?

3. Draw conclusions from each classification based on the answers to the questions

4. Compile a summary and link to waking behaviour if appropriate

Appendix F

Dream Interpretation: A Formal Analysis

1. **Write the dream report**

2. **Illogical thinking**

   How are the places shown as unreliable?

   How is the concept of time shown as irregular?

   How are the people shown as unreliable?

3. **Delusional beliefs**

   What do you believe or not believe about the dream content?

4. **Feelings**

   How did you feel during the dream?

   How did you feel on waking?

5. **The meaning of the dream**

   Sift out the illogical thinking and delusional beliefs.

   What is the rational part of the dream-self's behaviour?

   How is your behaviour connected to waking experience?

Appendix G

Dream Interpretation: The Integrative-Vision Model

1. **Write the dream report**

2. **Draw the dream (optional)**

3. **How does the dream setting connect to waking life experience?**

4. **How does the behaviour of the characters remind you of waking events?**

5. **What do the dream characters say to each other?**

6. **What are your thoughts?**

   Thoughts in your dream.

   How are these thoughts connected to waking life?

7. **What are your feelings?**

   Feelings in your dream.

   How are these feelings connected to waking life?

8. **What is the social referent of the dream (optional)?**

9. **An integration of the categories**

   Themes from dream experience.

   Themes from waking life experience.

10. **The meaning of the dream**

    What do the themes tell me about my current experience with these characters or objects and this situation?

11. **What action, if any, is required in waking life?**

Notes

1. Setting the Scene

1. "80 Red Beret Girls Revolt in the Rain," *Daily Express*, 1962, accessed Sept 16, 2016, http://www. *express.co.uk/paper-archive*. This report included reported a photograph of the "prime movers", including me, who staged a strike because we didn't want to wear our berets pulled down over our foreheads.

2. Stephanie Adam, *The Big Dream: A Qualitative Enquiry into Counsellor's Views of Selected Dream Models*, unpublished Doctoral Thesis, University of Manchester (2009), Joule Library Th 32644.

3. Illustration by Sarah Adam.

4. Illustration by Sarah Adam.

5. Richard Popkin and Avrum Stroll, *Philosophy Made Simple. The Theory of Knowledge* (Oxford, London, 1953), 215.

6. Artemidorous, *Oneirocritica: The Interpretation of Dreams* Trans. R White. (Torrance, Calif.: Original Books, 1975).

7. Robert L. Van de Castle, *Our Dreaming Mind* (London, Aquarian Press, 1994). 79.

8. William Harris Stahl, *Macrobius: Commentary on the Dream of Scipio* (New York: Columbia University Press, 1952).

9. Van de Castle, *Our Dreaming Mind*, 84.

10. Ibid., 87.

11. Iain Edgar, "Encountering the Dream: Intersecting Anthropological and Psychoanalytic Approaches," *Counselling and Psychotherapy Research, 3*, (2), (2003): 97. Original source Barbara Tedlock.

"Dreaming and Dream Research" in *Dreaming: Anthropological and Psychological Interpretations* (Cambridge University Press, 1987), 5.

12. Edgar, "Encountering the Dream: Intersecting Anthropological and Psychoanalytic Approaches", 97.

13. Micheal F. Brown, "Ropes of Sand: Order and Imagery in Aguaruna Dreams", 157, in Barbara Tedlock (ed) *Dreaming: Anthropological and Psychological Interpretations* (Cambridge University Press, 1987).

14. Ibid., 162.

15. Waud Kracke, "Myths in Dreams, Thoughts in Images: an Amazonian Contribution to the Psychoanalytic Theory of Primary Process", 33, in Barbara Tedlock (ed) *Dreaming: Anthropological and Psychological Interpretations* (Cambridge University Press, 1987).

16. Ibid., 33.

17. Kilton Stewart, "Dream Theory in Malaya," *Complex* (no. 6, 1951): 21–33.

18. Richard Gross, *Psychology: The Science of Mind and Behaviour* (London: Hodder & Stoughton, 2005), 245.

19. Brigitte Boothe, "The rhetorical organisation of dream telling" *Counselling and Psychotherapy Research* (1), (2), (2003): 106. Boothe claims that dreams don't contain the answers to "why," "what for," and "how so," which then creates a non-transparent space, because no-one is telling us why the dream events are happening.

20. Ibid., 106.

21. Ann Faraday, *The Dream Game* (New York: Harper & Row, 1974), 59. Faraday claims that A–Z dream books where dreamers look up the meaning of dream symbols, are counterproductive whether they are based on traditions, or modern psychological approaches.

22. Clara E. Hill, (ed), *Dream Work in Therapy. Facilitating Exploration, Insight and Action* (Washington: The American Psychological Association, 2004), 4. Hill states that standard dream dictionaries with their symbolic interpretations are unhelpful when applied without knowledge of the individual's associations.

23. Gayle Delaney, *Breakthrough Dreaming* (Bantam Books, New York, 1991), 237. Delaney says individuals should beware of interviewers who claims they know what your dream images mean thanks to their superior, wisdom into dream symbols.

24. Ibid., 4.

2. Dreams Reflect the Fulfilment of Unsatisfied Wishes

1. Helen Walker Pruner, *Sigmund Freud: His Life and Mind* (New Jersey: Transaction Publishers, 1992), 2.

2. Sigmund Freud. "Uber Coca" *Journal of Substance Abuse Treatment* Vol 1 (3), (1984): 206–217. First published 1884.

3. Illustration by Sarah Adam.

4. Sigmund Freud, *The Interpretation of Dreams* (New York: Oxford University Press, 1999, first published 1900).

5. Illustration by Barbara Lambert.

6. Illustration by Barbara Lambert.

7. Carlo Ginzburgh, "Morelli, Freud and Sherlock Holmes: Clues and Scientific Methods," *History Workshop Journal* 9, (1980): 8.

8. Freud, *The Interpretation of Dreams*, 85.

9. *Muriel's Wedding* a film released in 1994 about Muriel who wanted to have a glamorous wedding and to be removed from the dead-end town she lived in.

10. I liked The Dixie Chicks not only for their new brand of blue-grass music but also because the lead singer stood up to George Bush and challenged him openly about America's participation in the Iraq war.

11. "Wind Beneath My Wings" was recorded by a country and western singer Gary Morris in 1983, and later recorded by Bette Midler for the film *Beaches* in 1989.

12. John Dewey, *How We Think* (New York: D.C. Heath & Co, 1910), 57.

3. Dreams Are Words of Wisdom from Our Higher Selves

1.   Carl Gustav Jung, *Memories, Dreams, Reflections* (London: Fontana Press, 1995).

2.   Ibid., 67

3.   Ibid., 85.

4.   Ibid., 127.

5.   Ibid., 183.

6.   Ibid., 179–180.

7.   Ibid., 180.

8.   Ibid., 182.

9.   Illustration by Sarah Adam.

10. Jung, *Memories, Dreams, Reflections*, 184.

11. Richard Gross, *Psychology: The Science of Mind and Behaviour* (London: Hodder & Stoughton 2001), 133.

12. Illustration by Steph Adam.

13. Gayle Delaney, *Breakthrough Dreaming* (New York: Bantam Books, 1991), 49.

14. Barbara G. Walker, *The Women's Encyclopaedia of Myths and Secrets* (New York: Harper and Row, 1983), 244.

15. Arthur Conan Doyle, *The Hound of the Baskervilles* (London: Headline Publishing, 2006).

16. Ibid., 189.

17. Anthony Storr, *Jung* (London: Fontana Press, 1973), 80.

18. Carl Gustav Jung, *The Red Book* (London: W.W. Norton & Co, 2009).

19. Frederick L. Coolidge, *Dream Interpretation as a Psychotherapeutic Technique* (Seattle: Radcliffe Publishing, 2006), 72.

20. Ibid., 73.

21. Jung. *Memories, Dreams, Reflections*, 222.

22. Illustration by Sarah Adam.

23. Eugene Pascal, *Jung to Live By* (London; Souvenir Press, 1992), 259.

24. Barbara G. Walker, *The Women's Encyclopaedia of Myths and Secrets* (New York: Harper and Row, 1983), 695.

4. Dreams Are Fragmented Holes in Our Personalities

1. Petruska Clarkson and Jennifer Mackewn, *Fritz Perls Key Figures in Counselling and Psychotherapy Series* (London, Sage Publications, 1993), 3.

2. Frederick S. Perls, *In and Out the Garbage Pail* (California: Real People Press, 1969).

3. Frederick S, Perls, Ralph Hefferline, and Paul Goodman. *Gestalt Therapy: Excitement and Growth in the Human Personality* (Gouldsboro: Gestalt Journal Press Inc, 1951).

4. Illustration by Sarah Adam. This illustration is adapted from Ann Faraday's description in her book *Dream Power* (New York: Berkley Books, 1980 reprinted from 1972), 143, in which she claims that Perl's denied the existence of the unconscious. Instead, Faraday thought of Perls' concept of personality as a rubber ball revolving in the water, where only one section is visible at any given time. The therapist should work with the visible section in the context of the here-and-now therapeutic encounter.

5. Frederick S, Perls, "Counselling Gloria". There are several sites on YouTube to see this video.

6. Frederick S. Perls, *Gestalt Therapy Verbatim* (Gouldsboro: The Gestalt Journal Press, 1992), 3.

7. Ibid., 103.

8. Ibid., 103–106.

9. Ibid., 110.

10. "Nellie the Elephant" is a song I heard on the radio as a child during the 1950s. It tells of Nellie who packed her trunk and said goodbye to the circus. Off she went with a trumpety-trump to escape to the jungle. I think that Nellie was symbolic for me wanting to retire.

11. *Steptoe and Son* is a popular British television sitcom programme which I watched from 1962–1965.

12. Perls, *Gestalt Therapy Verbatim*, 24.

5. Interpretation from a Series of Dreams
Increases Self-Knowledge

1. Calvin S. Hall, *The Meaning of Dreams* (New York: Harper, 1953).

2. Calvin S. Hall and Vernon J. Nordby, *The Individual and His Dream* (New York: Signet, 1972).

3. Ibid., 158.

4. Ibid., 170.

5. Ibid., 167.

6. Ibid., 167.

7. Ibid., 168.

8. Ibid., 168.

9. Ibid., 168.

10. Ibid., 177.

11. Ibid., 175.

12. Ibid., 181.

13. Ibid., 182.

14. Ibid., 45.

15. Ibid., 50.

16. Ibid., 38.

17. Ibid., 175.

18. Ibid., 175.

19. Ibid., 175.

20. Leila Bright, *How to Interpret Dreams* (London: Hodder and Stoughton, 2013), 44.

6. Dreams Are Random Brain Activity

1. J. Allan Hobson, *Dream Life* (London: The MIT Press, 2011), 52.

2.   Ibid., 52.

3.   Ibid., 59.

4.   Ibid., 53.

5.   Ibid., 54.

6.   Eugine Aserinsky and Nathaniel Kleitman, "Regularly occurring periods of eye motility and concomitant phenomena during sleep," *Science* (1953): 273–274.

7.   J. Allan Hobson, *The Dreaming Brain* (New York: Basic Books, 1988).

8.   J. Allan Hobson, *Dreaming: A Very Short Introduction* (Oxford: Oxford University Press, 2002), 11.

9.   Ibid., 28.

10. Margie Patlak. "Dreams leave a wake-us-up call." http://www. Margiepatlak.co/dreams.pdf [accessed October 20 2016].

11. Farthing, William G, *The Psychology of Consciousness* (Englewood Cliffs: N.J: Prentice Hall, 1992), 298.

12. Hobson, *The Dreaming Brain,* 214.

13. Ibid., 5.

14. Inge Strauch and Barbara Meier, *In Search of Dreams* (Albany: State University of New York Press, 1996), 79.

15. The *St Trinian's* films were popular in the 1960s. My headmistress did not resemble the head of this school.

16. Hobson, *The Dreaming Brain,* 5.

17. Ibid., 212.

18. Inge Strauch and Barbara Meier, *In Search of Dreams,* 86.

19. Ibid., 86.

20. Stephen LaBerge, *Exploring the World of Lucid Dreams* (New York: Ballantine Books, 1994). LaBerge is one of the world's leading experts on lucid dreaming.

21. Hobson, *The Dreaming Brain,* 212.

22. Ibid., 7.

23. Inge Strauch and Barbara Meier, *In Search of Dreams*, 79.

24. Ibid., 95.

25. Hobson, *The Dreaming Brain*, 230.

26. J. Allan Hobson, *The Chemistry of Conscious States: Towards a Unified Model of the Brain and Mind* (New York: Little Brown and Co, 1996).

7. Dreams Are Visual Metaphors that Reflect our True Emotions

1. Stephanie Adam, *The Big Dream: A Qualitative Enquiry into Counsellor's Views of Selected Dream Models,* unpublished Doctoral Thesis, University of Manchester (2009), Joule Library Th 32644.

2. Stephen Paul and Geoff Pelham, "A Relational Approach to Therapy," in Stephen Palmer and Ray Woolfe (eds), *Integrative and Eclectic Counselling and Psychotherapy* (London: Sage, 2000), 110.

3. Ibid., 123.

4. Ann Faraday, *Dream Power* (New York: Berkley Books, 1980 reprinted from 1972).

5. Ann Faraday, *The Dream Game* (New York: Harper & Row, 1974).

6. Illustration by Sarah Adam and Barbara Lambert.

7. Ernest Hartmann, "Outline for a Theory on the Nature and Functions of Dreaming," *Dreaming* 6: 2, (1996): 148.

8. Ibid., 149.

9. Ibid., 149.

10. Ernest Hartmann, *The Nature and Functions of Dreaming* (New York: Oxford University Press, 2014), 54.

11. Montague Ullman, "A Note on the Social Referents of Dreams," *Dreaming,* Vol, 11: 1), (2001): 4.

12. Montague Ullman, "Dreams, the Dreamer and Society," In Gayle Delaney (ed), *New Directions in Dream Interpretation* (Albany: State University of New York Press), 36.

13. Ibid., 37.

14. K. R. Stewart, "Dream Theory in Malaya," *Complex*, 6 (1951): 21–33.

15. Patricia Garfield, *Creative Dreaming* (New York: Ballantyne Books, 1974).

16. Ibid., 101.

17. Ibid., 105.

18. Ibid., 90.

19. Faraday, *The Dream Game*, 260.

20. Ann Faraday and John Wren-Lewis, "The Selling of the Senoi," *Dream Network Bulletin* 3–4 (March–April 1984): 2.

21. G. William Domhoff. http://psych.ucsc.edu/dreams/Library/senoi5. html [accessed November 5 2016].

22. G. William Domhoff. *The Mystique of Dreams: A Search for Utopia through Senoi Dream Theory* (California: University of California Press, 1992).

23. Ibid., 17.

24. Ibid., 19.

25. Ibid., 62. Original source, K.R. Stewart, "Dream Theory in Malaya," 27.

26. Ibid., 62. Original source, K.R. Stewart, *Magico-Religious Beliefs and Practices in Primitive Society – A Sociological Interpretation of Their Therapeutic Aspects*, unpublished Ph.D. dissertation, London School of Economics, 1946: 151–152.

27. Illustration by Barbara Lambert.

28. Johnathan Smith, Paul Flowers and Michael Larkin, *Interpretive Phenomenological Analysis: Theory, Method and Research* (London: Sage publications, 2009).

8. Summing-Up of the Theories

1. Sigmund Freud, *The Interpretation of Dreams* (New York: Oxford University Press, 1999, first published 1900).

2.   Carl Gustav Jung, *Memories, Dreams, Reflections* (London: Fontana Press, 1995).

3.   Frederick S. Perls, *Gestalt Therapy Verbatim* (Gouldsboro: The Gestalt Journal Press, 1992).

4.   Calvin S. Hall and Vernon J. Nordby, *The Individual and His Dream* (New York: Signet, 1972), 175.

5.   Stephanie Adam, *The Big Dream – A Qualitative Enquiry into Counsellor's Views of Selected Dream Models,* unpublished Doctoral Thesis, University of Manchester (2009), Joule Library Th 32644.

6.   J. Allan Hobson, *The Dreaming Brain* (New York: Basic Books, 1988).

7.   Elizabeth, M. Thornton, "Does the unconscious mind really exist?" in Colin Feltham (ed). *Controversies in Psychotherapy and Counselling* (London: Sage, 1999), 19.

8.   Johnathan Smith, Paul Flowers and Michael Larkin, *Interpretive Phenomenological Analysis: Theory, Method and Research* (London: Sage, 2009).

9. A Readers Do–It–Yourself Model

1.   Stephen Paul and Geoff Pelham, "A Relational Approach to Therapy," in Stephen Palmer and Ray Woolfe, *Integrative and Eclectic Counselling and Psychotherapy* (London: Sage, 2000) 110.

2.   http:// www.asdreams.org.

3.   Ann Faraday, *Dream Power* (New York: Berkley Books, 1980 reprinted from 1972).

4.   Ann Faraday, *The Dream Game* (New York: Harper & Row, 1974).

5.   Calvin S. Hall and Vernon J. Nordby, *The Individual and His Dream* (New York: Signet, 1972).

6.   Gayle Delaney, *Breakthrough Dreaming* (Bantam Books, New York: Bantam Books, 1991).

7.   Eugine Gendlin, T, *Let Your Body Interpret Your Dreams* (Illinois: Chiron Publications, 1986

Bibliography

Adam Stephanie. *The Big Dream: A Qualitative Enquiry into Counsellor's Views of Selected Dream Models*. Unpublished Doctoral Thesis, University of Manchester, School Management Joule Library Th 32644, 2009.

Adam, Steph. *The Big Dream: A Qualitative Enquiry into Counsellor's Views of Selected Dream Models*. Unpublished paper presented at the 39th Society for Psychotherapy Research annual meeting, Barcelona, Spain, 18–21 June, 2008.

Adam, Steph. *Therapists, Clients and Dreams – What Next?* Work in Progress presented at the 11th British Association for Counselling and Psychotherapy Conference, Nottingham, 20 May 2005.

Adam, Steph and Fenia Christodoulidi. *The Use of Metaphor, Art and Poetry as an Agent in the Qualitative Research Process*. Unpublished paper presented at The Student Research *Conference, University* of Manchester Business School, 22 March 2009.

Artemidorus. *Oneirocritica: The Interpretation of Dreams*. Trans. R. White. Torrance Calif: Original Books, 1975.

Aserinsky, Eugine and Nathaniel Kleitman. "Regularly Occurring Periods of Eye Motility and Concomitant Phenomena during Sleep." *Science* (1953): 273–274. http:// www.asdreams.org.

Boothe, Brigitte. "The Rhetorical Organisation of Dream Telling." *Counselling and Psychotherapy Research* 1 (2) (2003): 101–113.

Bright, Leila. *How to Interpret Dreams*. London: Hodder and Stoughton, 2013.

Brown, Michael F. *"Ropes of Sand: Order and Imagery in Aguaruna Dreams."* In *Dreaming: Anthropological and Psychological Interpretations*. Edited by Barbara Tedlock. Cambridge: Cambridge University Press: 1987, 154–170.

Cardwell, Mike, Liz Clark, and Claire Meldrum. *Psychology*. London: Collins, 2004.

Clarkson, Petruska, and Jennifer Mackewn. *Fritz Perls Key Figures in Counselling and Psychotherapy Series*. London: Sage Publications, 1993.

Coolidge, Frederick L. *Dream Interpretation as a Psychotherapeutic Technique*. Abingdon, Oxon: Radcliffe Publishing Ltd, 2006.

Delaney, Gayle. *Breakthrough Dreaming*. New York: Bantam Books, 1991.

Dewey, John. *How We Think*. New York: D.C. Heath & Co, 1910.

Domhoff, G. William. http://psych.ucsc.edu/dreams/Library/senoi5.html [accessed Nov 5, 2016].

Domhoff, G.W. *The Scientific Study of Dreams*. Washington: American Psychological Association, 2003.

Domhoff, G.W. "A New Neurocognitive Theory of Dreams." *Dreaming*, 11 (1) (2001): 13-33.

Domhoff, G. W. *Finding Meaning in Dreams: A Quantitative Approach*. New York: Plenum Press, 1996.

Domhoff, G. William. *The Mystique of Dreams: A Search for Utopia through Senoi Dream Theory*. California: University of California Press, 1992.

Doyle, Arthur Conan. *The Hound of the Baskervilles*. London: Headline Publishing, 2006.

Edgar, Iain. "Encountering the Dream: Intersecting Anthropological and Psychoanalytic Approaches." *Counselling and Psychotherapy Research, 3* (2) (2003): 95–101.

"80 Red Beret Girls Revolt in the Rain." *Daily Express* Accessed Sept 16, 2016.http://www. express.co.uk/paper-archive

Faraday, Ann. *The Dream Game*. New York: Harper & Row, 1974.

Faraday, Ann. *Dream Power*. New York: Berkley Books, 1980-reprinted from 1972.

Faraday, Ann, and John Wren-Lewis. "The Selling of the Senoi." *Dream Network Bulletin*, (March-April 1984): 3-4.

Farthing, William G. *The Psychology of Consciousness*. Englewood Cliffs, N.J: Prentice Hall, 1992.

Freud, Sigmund. *The Interpretation of Dreams*. New York: Oxford University Press, 1999.

Freud, Sigmund. "Uber Coca," *Journal of Substance Abuse Treatment*, vol 1, (3), (1984): 206–217.

Freud, Sigmund. "Fragment of an Analysis of a Case of Hysteria." In *Standard Edition of the Complete Psychological Works of Sigmund Freud*, vol, 7, edited by J. Strachey, 7–121. London: The Hogarth Press, 1953.

Garfield, Patricia. *Creative Dreaming*. New York: Ballantine Books, 1974.

Gendlin, Eugine T. *Let Your Body Interpret Your Dreams*. Illinois: Chiron Publications, 1986.

Ginzburgh, Carlo. "Morelli, Freud and Sherlock Holmes: Clues and Scientific Methods." *History Workshop Journal,* 9 (1980): 5–36.

Gross, Richard. *Psychology: The Science of Mind and Behaviour*. London: Hodder and Stoughton, 2001.

Hall, Calvin. *The Meaning of Dreams*. New York: Harper, 1953.

Hall, Calvin S., and Vernon J. Nordby. *The Individual and his Dreams*. New York: Signet, 1972.

Hall, Calvin S. and Robert L. Van de Castle. *The Content Analysis of Dreams*. New York: Appleton Century Crofts, 1966.

Hall, James A. *Patterns of Dreaming*. Boston: Shambala, 1991.

Hartmann, Ernest. *The Nature and Functions of Dreaming*. New York: Oxford University Press, 2014.

Hartmann, Ernest. "Outline for a Theory on the Nature and Functions of Dreaming." *Dreaming* vol 6, no. 2 (1996): 147–170.

Hill, Clara E. (ed). *Dream Work in Therapy. Facilitating Exploration, Insight and Action*. Washington: The American Psychological Association, 2004.

Hobson, J. Allan. *Dream Life*. London: The MIT Press, 2011.

Hobson, J. Allan. *Dreaming: A Very Short Introduction*. Oxford: Oxford University Press, 2002.

Hobson, J. Allan. *The Chemistry of Conscious States: Towards a Unified Model of the Brain and Mind*. New York: Little Brown and Co, 1996.

Hobson, J. Allan. *The Dreaming Brain*. New York: Basic Books, 1988.

Jung, C. G. *The Red Book*. London: W.W. Norton & Co, 2009.

Jung, C. G. *Memories, Dreams, Reflections*. London: Fontana Press, 1995.

Kelsey, Morton T. *Dreams: The Dark Speech of the Spirit*. New York: Double Day, 1968.

Kracke, Waud. *"Myths in Dreams, Thoughts in Images: An Amazonian Contribution to The Psychoanalytic Theory of Primary Process."* In *Dreaming: Anthropological and Psychological Interpretations*, edited by Barbara Tedlock, 31-54. Cambridge: Cambridge University Press, 1987.

LaBerge, Stephen. *Exploring the World of Lucid Dreams*. New York: Ballantine Books, 1994.

Lakoff, George. "How Metaphor Structures Dreams: The Theory of Conceptual Metaphor Applied to Dream Analysis." *Dreaming*, vol 3, no. 2, (1993): 77–98.

McGinn, Colin. "Can We Solve the Mind–Body Problem?" *Mind,* New Series, vol 98, 391 (Jul, 1989): 349–366.

Paul, Stephen and Geoff Pelham. "A Relational Approach to Therapy." In *Integrative and Eclectic Counselling and Psychotherapy,* edited by Stephen Palmer, and Ray Woolfe, 110–126. London: Sage, 2000.

Pascall, Eugene. *Jung to Live By*. New York: Souvenir Press, 1992.

Patlak, Margie. "Dreams Leave a Wake-Us-Up Call." http://www.Margiepatlak.co/dreams.pdf [accessed Oct 20, 2016].

Perls, Frederick S. *Gestalt Therapy Verbatim*. Gouldsboro: Gestalt Journal Press Inc, 1992.

Perls, Frederick S. *In and Out the Garbage Pail*. California: Real People Press. 1969.

Perls, Frederick S. *Gestalt Therapy Verbatim*. Utah: The Real People Press, 1969.

Perls, Frederick S, Ralph Hefferline, and Paul Goodman. *Gestalt Therapy: Excitement and Growth in the Human Personality*. Gouldsboro: Gestalt Journal Press Inc, 1951.

Popkin, Richard H. and Avrum Stroll. *Philosophy Made Simple*. Oxford: Made Simple Books an imprint of Elsevier, 1993.

Rasmussen, Brian M. "Linking Metaphor and Dreams in Clinical Practice." *Psychoanalytic Social Work* vol. 9, no. 2 (2002): 71–87.

Smith Johnathan, Paul Flowers, and Michael Larkin. *Interpretive Phenomenological Analysis: Theory, Method and Research*. London: Sage publications, 2009.

Solms, Mark. "Dreams and Sleep are controlled by Different Brain mechanisms." *Behavioural and Brain Sciences* 23, no.6 (2000): 793–1121.

Stahl, William Harris. *Microbus: Commentary on the Dream of Scipio by Macrobius*. New York: Columbia University Press, 1952.

Stewart, K.R. "Dream Theory in Malaya." *Complex,* no. 6, (1951): 21–33.

Stewart, K.R. *Magico-Religious Beliefs and Practices in Primitive Society – A Sociological Interpretation of Their Therapeutic Aspects*, Unpublished PhD dissertation, London School of Economics, 1946.

Storr, Anthony. *Jung*. London: Fontana Press, 1973.

Strauch Inge and Barbara Meier. *In Search of Dreams*. Albany: State University of New York Press, 1996.

Tedlock, Barbara. "Dreaming and Dream Research." In *Dreaming: Anthropological and Psychological Interpretations,* edited by Barbara Tedlock, 1–30. Cambridge University Press, 1987.

Thornton, Elizabeth M. "Does the Unconscious Mind Really Exist?" In *Controversies in Psychotherapy and Counselling,* edited by Colin Feltham, 7–14. London: Sage, 1999.

Ullman, Montague. "A Note on the Social Referents of Dreams." *Dreaming,* vol 11, no.1 (2001): 1–12.

Ullman, Montague. "Dreams, the Dreamer and Society." In *New Directions in Dream Interpretation,* edited by Gayle Delaney, 36–40. Albany: State University of New York Press, 1993.

Ullman, Montague. "The Social Roots of the Dream." *American Journal of Psychoanalysis.* vol 20, 2, (1960): 180–196.

Van de Castle, Robert L. *Our Dreaming Mind.* New York: Aquarian, 1994.

Walker, Barbara G. *The Woman's Encyclopaedia of Myths and Secrets.* New York: Harper and Row, 1983.

Walker, Pruner Helen. *Sigmund Freud: His Life and Mind.* New Jersey: Transaction Publishers, 1992.

Index

action stage in dreams, 87, 116
activation stage, 91
activation-synthesis theory, 88, 91
active imagination, 41-42, 121
active reflection, 24
Adam, Steph, 1-2, 102-103, 124
aggressive interactions, 64, 80
Aguaruna tribe, 7
amnesia, 9, 92
amplification, 33, 120
anxiety, 15, 47, 49-50, 121
archetypal association, 38, 120
Aserinsky, Eugine, 90
auditory hallucinations, 29

Beatty, Chester, 6
behaviour, 106, 122
Boothe, Brigitte, 11
brain, 89
bull-shit, 48, 121

central image, 107
Charcot, Jean, 13
chicken-shit, 48, 121
collective unconscious, 32, 40, 120
compensatory function of dreams, 30
condensation, 17, 119
conscience, 116
conscious, 15
consciousness, 31
content analysis, 62
content features of dreams, 2
cultural association, 37, 120

day residue, 20
death wish, 31
Delaney, Gayle, 11
delusional beliefs, 92, 96, 98, 123
Descartes, 3-5, 89
dialogue in dreams, 106, 114
displacement, 17, 119
Domhoff, Bill, 110-111
Doyle, Arthur, Conan, 18, 38
drawing, 35, 112
dream
    bizzareness, 11

definition of, 2
journals, 9, 129-137
realities, 5
dream-work, 16, 119
dualism, 89

Edgar, Iain, 7, 111
Egyptians, 6
electroencephalograph (EEG), 90
elephant-shit, 48, 121
emotions, 33-34, 62, 65, 92, 96, 99, 121, 123-124
Esalen Institute, 50

Faraday, Ann, 11, 103, 109
Fleisch-Marxow, 14, 21
forebrain, 92
formal features of dreams, 3, 92
fragmented holes, 49, 52, 121
free association, 18, 119
Freud, Sigmund, 12, 13, 119, 125
friendly interactions, 64, 81

Garfield, Patricia, 109-110
genetic traits, 14
Gestalt therapy, 46

Hall, Calvin, 12, 123, 125
hallucinations, 2, 90, 93
Hartmann, Ernest, 106-107
here-and-now, 47, 122
Hill, Clara, 11
Hobson, J. Allan, 12, 88, 123, 125
hot-seat, 50
hypnogogic, 90
hypnopompic, 91
hypnosis, 13-14
hysteria, 14, 19-20,

illogical thinking, 92, 94, 96, 123
impasse, 50, 55, 60, 67
individuation, 40, 121
insight, 19, 24-25, 60, 99-100, 120
Integrative – Vision Model, 103-104, 112, 124

About the Author

Steph Adam is a retired counsellor with over twenty years' experience of working with adults, couples and young people aged 16–21 years, encompassing a wide range of issues. She started studying the benefits of dreams as a therapeutic tool at the University of Manchester, whilst undertaking a Doctorate degree. Recently, she has extended some of her research to the general reader, resulting in this publication. She lives in York with her dog Daisy, where she spends time with family and friends. She is currently studying creative writing, military history and foreign languages. You can find out more about Steph at www.stephadam.co.uk